CW01460303

WHAT IS PTSD?

3 STEPS TO HEALING TRAUMA

BY

DR. ANNA BARANOWSKY
&
TERESA LAUER, LMHC

WHAT IS PTSD?

3 STEPS TO HEALING TRAUMA

By Dr. Anna B. Baranowsky, Ph.D., C.Psych. & Teresa Lauer, MA, LMHC

© 2012, 2013 CONTENTS

ISBN-13: 978-1478286738

ISBN-10: 1478286733

Dr. Anna B. Baranowsky is a clinical psychologist in Toronto and CEO of the Traumatology Institute. Anna specializes in post-trauma care and has dedicated her work to assisting trauma survivors, communities, and organizations after critical events. She offers comprehensive Trauma Training and Compassion Fatigue Resiliency programs on-line and on-site. For information about the Traumatology Institute Training Curriculum E-learning visit www.ticlearn.com. For in-class profess-ional training, visit www.psychink.com.

DR. ANNA B. BARANOWSKY, Traumatology Institute, CANADA

Teresa Lauer, MA, LMHC is a licensed psychotherapist in Redmond, Washington and founder of RapeRecovery.com. She has treated hundreds of clients suffering from Post-Traumatic Stress Disorder and associated social and intimate relationship difficulties. Teresa is the founder of www.RapeRecovery.com.

DEDICATION

DR. ANNA BARANOWSKY

There are many people who make it possible for me to do my work and to feel supported in my life. To start with, I am extremely privileged to work with people from all walks of life who have trusted me and allowed me to work with them in their trauma recovery. Every day I learn from those warriors on their healing journeys.

I am forever grateful for my father, who experienced immense tragedy yet remained kind and compassionate with everyone in his life, and to my mother who taught me about determination and inner strength; to my darling Chris, who is a wonderful companion and spouse, and to Cassie and Jasper, who have enriched my every waking day; to Gold and the Golds, who are special in my heart; to Zahava who demonstrated the beauty of a strong and intelligent woman; to my writers, masterminds, SYPS, everyone with T.I., Judit, Maureen and Aliza, to Eric whom has been instrumental in my growth, and, of course, to Teresa Lauer, who I have had the great joy of writing this book with. My heartfelt appreciation goes out to all of you in my life.

TERESA LAUER, LMHC

As with all my endeavors, this book, for me, would not be possible without my husband, Phil. No one could champion me more than you could and I humbly thank you for the love that you have shown me all of these years. Each day you remind me that trauma does not have to equal pain, but can be a rebirth to a life worth living. And thanks to my mother and father, who endured their traumas, but made sure that I didn't live a life of fear; I miss you both dearly.

To Anna, thank you for sharing this journey with me; I have enjoyed it immensely. Your dedication to the comfort and care of trauma victims is inspiring and admirable. Finally, to my clients, who have allowed me into their lives at their most vulnerable moments, I thank you and honor your courage and faith that there is good in the world.

TABLE OF CONTENTS

SECTION 1
IMPACT AFTER TRAUMA

INTRODUCTION

WHAT IS PTSD?

PTSD stands for **P**ost-**T**raumatic **S**tress **D**isorder, which is an anxiety disorder that can occur following a traumatic event. A psychological trauma, as opposed to a physical trauma or injury, occurs when you experience an emotionally disturbing or distressing event. Although we commonly think of trauma as a reaction to a violent event or a terrible accident, we know that individuals can also experience emotional trauma after being physically injured or diagnosed with a serious illness.

During a traumatic event, you may have felt that your life, or the life of another, was in danger and that you had no control of the outcome. Even witnessing an event, in which someone died or was seriously injured, can cause PTSD symptoms and result in a diagnosis of it. It is not unusual for you to experience uncomfortable or upsetting memories of a traumatic event, as well as potentially strong physical reactions.

You may also experience uncomfortable or distressing emotions such as anger, fear, and helplessness. If these symptoms do not go away, or if they interfere with your daily activities or your enjoyment in life, it's time to seek help.

It is important to remember that only a qualified mental health professional can verify a diagnosis of PTSD through a series of clinical interviews and tests that inquire as to whether you have experienced specific symptom responses for at least one month.

3 ESSENTIAL STEPS TO HEALING TRAUMA

The following is an overview of the three essential steps to healing the trauma that we will address in this book, enabling you to master the skills necessary to begin and move forward in your trauma recovery.

STEP 1: FINDING COMFORT

Finding comfort and ensuring your safety is an integral part of healing the trauma and regaining, or claiming for the first time, a sense of safety within yourself. For this reason, self-care skills are paramount to recovery. We will focus a portion of the *Finding Comfort* section on presenting specially designed exercises to help you accomplish this goal. Building a foundation for increased confidence and self-esteem as well as building trust in your judgment begins with this step.

STEP 2: REMEMBERING YOUR TRAUMA

There is a sense of grief and loss in trauma. Life is not the same as before the event and you may feel that you have suffered a loss of innocence. Life is *supposed* to be fair, equitable and just – but this trauma may have shaken your core beliefs. This step is where your deeper work begins. Following your first step, you will be able to identify when you need self-soothing, and apply an approach that you have found to be effective in meeting your needs when feeling overwhelmed. This allows you to step back from your disturbing symptoms and gain perspective in their source. Recognizing your triggers to emotional and physical discomfort is a big step in recovery as it frees you up from reacting automatically and, instead, cues you to settle your emotions and bodily reactions before they feel out of control. This will be a powerful tool to use wherever you are. Having worked through your trauma history makes this much easier to accomplish. Remembering the trauma is the next important step in your healing. It is only half the task, however, talking about your trauma and integrating it into your life story is central to moving ahead.

STEP 3: BEGINNING TO LIVE AGAIN!

You will be ready to redefine yourself as a person who has experienced trauma in your history, and not as a trauma survivor. There is a profound difference between the two. Your trauma no longer defines who you are.   Instead, you have experienced a trauma, learned from it and grown.

4

Despite your best efforts and your fervent wish that it had never happened, your trauma has had an effect on you. In this step, you will be preparing yourself to reconnect with important people in your life whether they are family, friends, colleagues, or community members – and, most importantly, with yourself in a new and profound way. You will be ready to redefine yourself and to seek a healthy existence through physical, intellectual, creative and personal growth. You will be ready to live again!

HOW TO BEST USE THIS BOOK

As mental health professionals, we use the Diagnostic and Statistical Manual of Mental Disorders (DSM) in our daily practice. You will see the DSM-5 referred to throughout our book as a guide used to describe symptoms, descriptions and other criteria pertaining to Post-Traumatic Stress Disorder (PTSD).

Please note that we have updated our book to reflect salient changes to the criteria for PTSD, most notably the addition of a fourth criteria *"Negative Cognition and Mood"* to the cluster of the original three symptoms.

Also please note that the naming convention of the DSM has been changed to reflect an updated numbering system, hence DSM-5, from the previous version of DSM-IV.

The goal of our book is to provide guidance through the healing of your trauma and to empower you. You should not forget the trauma but rather, learn how to find a healthy way to integrate it into your history so that it is no longer a problem. The goal of our book is to provide guidance through the healing of your trauma and to empower you. You should not forget the trauma but rather, learn how to find a healthy way to integrate it into your history so that it is no longer a problem.

Each of the three steps that we outlined above (*Finding Comfort, Remembering Your Trauma,* and *Beginning to Live Again*) contain concepts critical to your recovery, following a number of exercises for self-soothing and for coping with your symptoms. The exercises can be found at the end of each section so that you may easily review them as required. It is important to note that recovery occurs in a circuitous – rather than linear – fashion. At times, you may feel as if you are taking one step forward and two steps back.

This is to be expected and there is nothing wrong with going back to the concepts and exercises even though you may have moved ahead in the book. Each exercise follows the same structure below:

- **Recovery Stories:** We have added recovery stories to illustrate the experiences of those we have worked with as well as their experiences with the exercises in the book. Please note that while we draw from our experiences of having treated thousands of clients, confidentiality is strictly maintained at all times. Our hope is that you will be inspired by our clients to realize that healing from your trauma can be a reality!

- **Goal:** You will notice that each exercise has a goal section so that you can reflect on our desired outcome when working with the exercises.

- **Time Out:** Time out refers to any contraindications for the exercise; for instance, if you are experiencing any dissociation, or if you feel overwhelmed and need a break. This will signal a need to go slower, to return to Step I exercises, to take a walk, to listen to some music or to speak with a support person in your life until you find that sense of steady calm again and feel ready to work through the next step or exercise. Your safety is of the utmost importance.

- **Materials and Layout:** This indicates whether additional materials are needed to complete the exercise. We have placed some additional forms on www.WhatIsPTSD.com/forms for you to download. This is more important for those using e-readers or electronic versions of the book as the downloadable forms will give you a paper template to complete the exercises.

- **Path to Complete:** Here you will find the detailed instructions to complete each exercise.

TYPES OF TRAUMA

There are several types of trauma, but we will be focusing on what we call, *Type I* and *Type II*, categorized by the circumstance in which the trauma occurred.

TYPE I TRAUMA

Type I traumas are singular events that are overwhelming and unexpected, leaving you with feelings of horror and fear. Treatment for Type I traumas is very effective if provided shortly after the event. Type I traumatic events include:

- Serious accidents including car accidents, plane crashes and significant sporting accidents, etc.
- Natural disasters including earthquake, fire, tornado, hurricane and floods, etc.
- Acts of violence, such as a physical assault, mugging, or rape, that are viewed as unusual and not a constant threat
- Terrorist attacks that are limited in scope and viewed as a one-time event

TYPE II TRAUMA

Type II traumas are expected, but unavoidable events that are sustained over a period of time, such as:

- Combat or military experiences, including blasts and the witnessing of injury or death of fellow soldiers
- Repetitive physical or sexual abuse
- Childhood abuse or incest
- Workplace harassment or bullying at school
- Terrorist attacks that come with a threat of repeated actions

YOUR RESPONSE TO TRAUMA

There are certain responses that all trauma survivors experience (like feeling helpless and fearful) no matter the type of trauma or whether they were the ones injured in the event.

The intensity of these symptoms varies based on a number of factors like:

- Whether you were the one who was directly affected
- Whether the person who passed away or was severely injured was someone whom you had a close relationship with
- How long and intense the traumatic event lasted
- How close you were to the traumatic event
- How much you felt in control of the event
- How quickly you received help after the event

Experiencing Post-Traumatic symptoms that you cannot manage is an early warning sign that your coping skills are no longer working effectively. This is especially true if it has been longer than one month since the incident occurred. For some people, many years can go by before they reach out for help, leaving the survivors feeling overwhelmed and unable to manage their lives in the best possible way. A diagnosis of Acute Stress Disorder is appropriate for symptoms that are resolved within a month.

TRAUMA RESPONSE CHECKLIST

The following exercise is to be used in conjunction with our book, *"What Is PTSD? 3 Steps to Healing Trauma"* for best effect. Please visit our website, www.WhatIsPTSD.com for additional resources.

The checklist below was developed as a brief screening instrument. It will not provide a diagnosis but rather is an indicator for you to consider the areas of strain you have experienced after traumatic exposure. Read each of the statements and select the box that best applies to you in the past month.

Trauma Response Checklist (Baranowsky, 2013)

Event Question

Did you believe that the event could result in death or physical injury to you or another?   ☐ Yes ☐ No

Answer the following questions based your experiences in the last four weeks, or since the incident.

Distress/Strain Questions

1. I have difficulty falling or staying asleep   ☐ Yes ☐ No

2. I notice I am more irritable or aggressive   ☐ Yes ☐ No

3. I have more difficulty concentrating   ☐ Yes ☐ No

4. I feel more on alert and watchful since the event(s)   ☐ Yes ☐ No

5. I startle easily (i.e., when I hear loud noises, sudden movements)   ☐ Yes ☐ No

6.   I engage more often in reckless or self-harming behavior   ❏ Yes ❏ No

Steer Clear Questions

1.   At times, I try to avoid thoughts or feelings related to the   ❏ Yes ❏ No
       experience(s)

2.   Sometimes I try to avoid activities or situations that remind   ❏ Yes ❏ No
       me of the event(s)

Negative Thoughts and Mood Questions

1.   I cannot remember all the important details of the event(s)   ❏ Yes ❏ No

2.   I experience persistent negative beliefs about myself, other   ❏ Yes ❏ No
       people, or the world (i.e., fear of dying early; I cannot trust
       others)

3.   I have more feelings of guilt since the event(s)   ❏ Yes ❏ No

4.   I often feel unhappy, angry, anxious or irritable since the   ❏ Yes ❏ No
       event(s)

5.   I am not as interested in participating in activities as I was   ❏ Yes ❏ No
       before the event(s)

6.   I have withdrawn or been more detached from others since   ❏ Yes ❏ No
       the event(s)

7.   I don't feel as happy as I used to before the event(s)   ❏ Yes ❏ No

Negative Interference Questions

1.   I feel emotionally upset when exposed to reminders of the   ❏ Yes ❏ No
       event(s)

2.   I experience unwanted thoughts, images or sensitivity to the   ☐ Yes ☐ No
        event(s)

3.   At times, I act or feel like a traumatic event is still happening   ☐ Yes ☐ No

4.   I experience dreams or nightmares related to the event(s)   ☐ Yes ☐ No

5.   I experience physical distress when exposed to reminders of   ☐ Yes ☐ No
        event(s) (i.e., body tension, nausea, rapid heart rate,
        rapid/shallow breathing, etc.)

Associated Disturbance Questions

1.   I have the desire to harm myself or another   ☐ Yes ☐ No

2.   I feel very helpless or hopeless   ☐ Yes ☐ No

3.   I feel like nothing will be good again   ☐ Yes ☐ No

4.   I am drinking or using drugs more often since the event(s)   ☐ Yes ☐ No

5.   I get more headaches, muscle tension, nausea and fear since   ☐ Yes ☐ No
        the event

SCORING FOR THE TRAUMA RESPONSE CHECKLIST

Trauma Response Checklist (TRC)

This instrument is broken up into six sections. The first five correspond directly with the DSM-5 diagnostic criterion for Post-Traumatic Stress Disorder. These include:

Event Question - Add one point for an answer of yes. One point is required to endorse the Event section.

Distress/Strain Questions - Add one point for each yes answer. A minimum of two points are required to endorse the Distress Strain section.

Steer Clear Questions - Add one point for each yes answer. A minimum of one point is required to endorse the Steer Clear section.

Negative Thoughts and Mood Questions - Add one point for each yes answer. A minimum of two points are required to endorse the Negative Thoughts and Mood section.

Negative Interference Questions - Add one point for each yes answer. A minimum of one point is required to endorse the Negative Interference section.

Associated Disturbance Questions - Add one point for each yes answer. Use caution if the respondent answered yes on questions 1, 2 or 4. A referral and special care are required in these cases, regardless of answers to any other questions on this instrument. Endorsement of the Associated Disturbance section occurs when 1, 2 or 4 are answered yes or a minimum of two yes answers are made.

Further Care & Referral Indicators: Endorsement of a minimum of five out of the six question categories above indicate further care and referrals. Endorsement of questions 1, 2 or 4 on the Associated Disturbance section alone indicates the need for special care and further referrals.

HOW THE BRAIN AND BODY WORK AFTER TRAUMA

Exciting new research is currently underway in the area of how the mind and body work in concert following a trauma, thus leading to new ways of treating symptoms. The Polyvagal Theory, developed by Dr. Stephen Porges, is one of the exciting new areas of research exploring the Mind-Body Connection. It highlights the importance of the regulation of heart rate in returning the body to homeostasis, a steady state of relaxed equilibrium, even in the midst of stress. Below is an overview of the Polyvagal Theory.

THE POLYVAGAL THEORY

This research is opening up a dynamic area of post-trauma care and holds the hope of recovery for trauma survivors. The Vagus Nerve can trigger a shutdown system in the body when we are exposed to a traumatic event that feels unmanageable. The Vagus Nerve is linked directly to heart rate variability or the beat-to-beat rhythm of our heart. When heart rate variability is too low, we can slip into a frozen state – similar to the deer-in-the-headlights response. If it gets too low we can experience dissociative states (to be explained in a later chapter) or have the sensation of being out of our bodies. Surprisingly, this is a helpful response that potentially removes us from direct exposure to extreme pain and suffering. It makes sense if we think of a defense system that starts with a calm steady state where we are enjoying comfortable connections with others as the standard starting point.

The next step is the preparation to respond to perceived danger in the following order: First, we try to fight or run away in response to danger, but if we cannot escape or fight, the body mind response is to freeze. This is a helpful response in circumstances where the threat is so overwhelming that potential death or extreme injury occurs within a numbing cloak. The real problem with this is that for survivors re-engaging in everyday life, lifting that cloak of numbness can feel difficult to accomplish. Some of the best ways to achieve this are to gradually expose ourselves to gentle social cues of safety such as the sound of a supportive friend's voice, an audio recording of a relaxation exercise, or music.

Other helpful social cues include: the look of support on another person's face, comforting words, soothing music and an environment that feels at ease and stable. Regulating our heart rate is a cornerstone of recovery according to the Polyvagal Theory. We will cover exercises in *Step 1: Finding Comfort* to help you learn to regulate your heart rate through breathing exercises and other approaches that we have found helpful with our clients. Whatever approach you use that feels helpful to you in your recovery – remember that we are wired for finding a sense of comfort within ourselves and if we search for it regularly, we will find it. The Polyvagal Theory reminds us to recognize a deep sense of calm and centered peacefulness as our birthright and our home base – learn to count on it.

THE MIND-BODY CONNECTION

There are several areas of the brain that have tremendous influence over our subsequent thoughts and actions following trauma. Let's look at several of these areas below and how some of these systems work in concert and how we can use this information to encourage the healing process.

THE AMYGDALA

The Amygdala acts as an emotional control center in our brains and helps us to instantly feel certain emotions; those that we feel in ourselves and those that we perceive in others. When we feel fear, we know that the Amygdala is actively engaged in the brain. The Amygdala is responsible for our ability to respond rapidly to signs of danger and to activate and mobilize all resources to fight, flight, or freeze as a response to this danger. This works well with trauma survivors but once this neural pathway is engaged in serious situations it is not always easy to turn it off or lower the stress volume. This is why you may experience a lack of sleep or hyper-vigilance long after the danger is over. The Amygdala response can occur so quickly that we do not have time to confirm that our early warning signs of danger are correct. Hence, trauma survivors may respond with anger, fear, or a startle when there is no current source of danger igniting the reaction.

THE HIPPOCAMPUS

The Hippocampus stores memories so that in the future if you have a need to respond to danger, you are prepared to recall triggers and prepare your mind and body for rapid response to threat. This results in the release of Cortisol, the stress hormone that can interfere with memory and produce an automatic fearful response to danger signs. It is easy to see how useful this system can be when we are trying to respond quickly to true danger, but it can backfire when we are continually responding long after the danger has passed. When you store the traumatic memories of your experience, they are stored along with the strong emotions that occurred at the time as well, so any time you experience a trigger of this memory, you may also experience strong emotions (i.e., upset, agitation, anger, fear, confusion) as well. So there is no surprise that one of the key features of PTSD is the avoidance of any triggers to the traumatic memory. But as life will have it, we are constantly exposed to reminders and working through our stories on our journeys to recovery is the best route to a better life experience.

THE SENSORY THALAMUS

The next thing to add to this picture is the Sensory Thalamus, responsible for gathering information. Part of this new information is sent directly to the Amygdala to determine whether the alarm system should be activated and mobilized. Information is also concurrently sent to the Sensory Cortex to assess and confirm meaning (this is the slow route and is more analytical and reflective). However, by this time, the Amygdala may have already set off the alarm bells of the Autonomic Nervous System's SNS. Once this happens, we are into our reaction and may be sweating, tense, breathing quickly and agitated before we are able to confirm that a threat has occurred.

THE SYMPATHETIC NERVOUS SYSTEM

The Sympathetic Nervous System (known as the SNS) is a part of your nervous system that is responsible for accelerating your heart rate, constricting blood vessels and raising your blood pressure. The SNS, along with the Parasympathetic Nervous System (PNS) makes up the Autonomic Nervous System, the branch of the nervous system that performs involuntary functions. Once the SNS is engaged to fight, flight or freeze, the more reflective information processing that occurs in the Sensory Cortex is short-circuited. So, you may feel as if you have overreacted after the event, but while you're in the middle of a response and feeling angry, startled, or fearful, you are fully engaged and your response may feel entirely realistic and justified for the situation you feel you are in. The goal is always to bring yourself back to a stable base in your comfort zone – reengaging the Parasympathetic Nervous System (known for its rest and digest ability) and engaging the Vagus Nerve to return you to the inner calm steady state that you have hardwired as a part of your core functioning. When the SNS is engaged, all your energy is moved to activate a *get-out-of-danger* impulse and away from the normal digestive functioning, the warming of fingers and toes, and the management of other bodily functions that are not critical for survival. So it makes sense that after a traumatic event, you might have a stomachache, lose your appetite, feel cold or exhausted.

CORTISOL – THE STRESS HORMONE

Emotional and physical strain can release a cascade of chemicals into the body and mind. Some of these chemicals, like Cortisol, can have a big impact on how we function after trauma. After exposure to a disturbing event, the body and mind send signals that activate the adrenal glands, which pump out high levels of the stress hormone, Cortisol.

Too much Cortisol short-circuits the cells in the hippocampus, making it harder to organize the memory of the trauma or stressful experience. Memories lose their context and become fragmented.

These fragments can become re-ignited whenever something reminds us of our trauma, resulting in another big Cortisol release. Once high levels of Cortisol are released, it makes it difficult to find a sense of relaxation. This is a part of the response chain that can create strong emotional reactions even in safe circumstances leaving us feeling overwhelmed, depleted and shaken up by trauma reminders. It also reminds us that finding calm after trauma is a necessity and not a luxury item.

WHEN IT FEELS LIKE NOTHING IS REAL: THIS IS DISSOCIATION

There are times when the memories and feelings surrounding a traumatic event are just too much for the survivor to bear and so they simply break away from consciousness; some in minor ways, some more serious such as Dissociative Disorder where the personality splits off, experiencing a disconnect between the mind (conscious awareness) and body. This dissociation can appear while the trauma is occurring as well as afterwards. Below are some of the varying types of dissociation that can occur along with PTSD. Dissociation is especially prevalent in traumatic events occurring in childhood abuse or trauma that is particularly extreme in nature.

EMOTIONAL NUMBING

Emotional numbing is a type of dissociation that occurs where the only feelings present after a trauma is a sense of emotional numbness. In these cases, memories may remain fully intact, but there are no associated feelings attached to the experience.

DISSOCIATIVE FUGUE

You have probably read stories in the paper where a person went missing and was later found miles away, unable to remember how they got there. This is a dissociative fugue; an unexplained, sudden travel with confusion about how it occurred.

DEPERSONALIZATION

Depersonalization is the sense of not being in your body. One client explained this as being in the corner of the ceiling and watching herself in the therapy session. She didn't feel she was "within" her body at the time; others have described it as having an "out of body" experience or watching their lives as if it were a movie.

DISSOCIATIVE AMNESIA

Dissociative Amnesia is the inability to remember information that is beyond typical forgetfulness and often has to do with the details of a traumatic event.

DISSOCIATIVE IDENTITY DISORDER

Previously known as Multiple Personality Disorder, many people were first introduced to Dissociative Identity Disorder through the classic movie *Sybil*, the true story of a woman who experienced a traumatic childhood, developing 13 separate personalities. Dissociative Identity Disorder is one of the most severe forms of the dissociative disorders and is characterized by personalities suddenly coming to the fore when the individual is under extreme stress.

Learning and mastering the skills necessary to self-sooth are critical so that dissociation occurs with lessening intensity and frequency.

HOW TO STAY PRESENT IN HEALING TRAUMA

It is important to stay present in all activities, of course, but staying present during your healing is critical to your well-being. Although dissociation is a technical term that occurs when the brain is overwhelmed with emotional, physiological and cognitive stimuli, it is a symptom that can interfere with your recovery and needs to be addressed. Dissociation is a form of escape when the trauma becomes too over-whelming for you to handle. Dissociation keeps you from being able to remain present in the moment and working through your trauma history. It also keeps you in a state of unconscious responding, which means that you are not fully aware and conscious of your life choices.

Living purposefully means being present in the moment, fully engaged in your life, rather than being reactive and disengaged. We will present exercises and vignettes to help you stay grounded while you practice new skills at gaining and retaining control, both in your body and your surroundings.

FINDING A TRAUMA THERAPIST

We recognize that books can be a helpful first step, but that a more guided approach is essential for some in their recovery. Anna has developed a groundbreaking website specifically to help trauma survivors find and connect with skilled trauma therapists.

TraumaLine1 is a comprehensive resource where, as a survivor of trauma, you are able to fully explore your potential therapist's background, education, treatment approaches, specialties and more.

Also, you will find E-therapy and Online counseling resources to provide assistance even if you cannot find help in your community. Please visit www.whatisptsd.com and www.TraumaLine1.com for these valuable resources.

You will find if you choose to seek out and work with a skilled trauma therapist that this person can be central to your continued healing, long after therapy has ended. Compassion and therapy are key components, so when selecting a trauma therapist, research the depth of work that they have done in the treatment of trauma, the type of treatment in which they specialize and their level of success. A trauma-informed therapist can open a window into understanding how you feel about yourself and your trauma history.

Along with being a premiere "matching service", TraumaLine1 provides a wealth of information and articles addressing subjects such as bullying, treatment approaches like EMDR (Eye Movement Desensitization and Reprocessing) and more.

Visit www.TraumaLine1.com today to learn more or to search for a trauma therapist in your area. Remember that many of the therapists on TraumaLine1 work with newer methods of E-Counseling or Telephone Counseling, so even if there is no one available locally, you might be able to find a skilled Trauma Therapist who can help you from afar.

Visit www.whatisptsd.com for more information about options.

HEALING WITH NEW ENERGY

It is important to know that no matter how long ago your trauma occurred, or where you are at emotionally, it is not too late to begin your recovery. If after reading this book, you feel you are ready for a more directed approach, please remember there are people willing to support you, as well as professionals, with expertise in the treatment of trauma, who have the compassion and empathy to assist in your healing process.

Remember, no matter how lonely you feel you are *not* alone. There are thousands of people who understand what you have been through, along with care providers who have dedicated their professional training to help you.

Our hope for you is the opportunity to begin your recovery with "What is PTSD" and wish you a good journey into *Step One: Finding Comfort*.

SECTION 2
STEP 1: FINDING COMFORT

CHAPTER 1   THE IMPORTANCE OF FINDING COMFORT

In working with thousands of trauma survivors, we understand that even the thought of experiencing comfort again might be difficult to imagine. Yet achieving comfort is crucial to your recovery. Without this, it is almost impossible to safely progress toward trauma recovery. Since this is really the goal, we need to start with "Finding Comfort".

So what is "Finding Comfort" about? It is about the skills that help you relax and settle down the emotional strain, the physical tension, and the busy talk in our minds. This prepares us on all levels to face our traumatic history and gives us the sturdiness to work through what has occurred.

A trauma is an abnormal situation for which no one is prepared. We can feel overwhelmed and hopeless after a trauma and become convinced that things will never get better. However, we know that traumatic stress treatments work. We know that exposure to fearful memories is a critical element to the treatment and is an essential part of recovery.

GOALS FOR STEP 1: FINDING COMFORT

1. Ensuring you are safe from danger

2. Learning about the four clusters of trauma symptoms that can affect your day-to-day living: Re-experiencing, Avoidance and Numbing, Negative Cognition and Mood and Hyperarousal

3. Mastering the goals for managing these traumatic symptoms now, while in the midst of healing, and in the future

4. Gaining knowledge into the four primary ways to reconnect with others through physical, intellectual, creative, and personal growth

5. Applying your new skills daily

FINDING COMFORT WITHIN

Safety is the overriding goal of your first step towards beginning to live again after the trauma. Developing awareness of what is happening emotionally, physically and psychologically following an abnormal situation such as a trauma is imperative to your healing.

We know that people process the experience differently, based on their history, perceptions, body physiology, genetics and emotions. Therefore, each individual will have a unique ability to tolerate exposure to their traumatic memories and will need to move at their own pace. We want to walk with you as you progress through your journey toward recovery after trauma.

ENSURING YOU ARE SAFE FROM DANGER

Your feelings of safety relate to arousal symptoms, first experienced during your trauma. While it is important to listen to your instincts in order to keep yourself safe in all circumstances, certain feelings may be in response to a perceived threat, rather than real danger at that particular moment. In these situations, we encourage you to ask: *"Are these feelings signaling danger based on my trauma or am I experiencing real danger?"* Let's take a moment to explore the difference – and why it exists:

Danger in your environment is very real, especially in cases of combat or domestic violence where your surroundings are keeping you unsafe, for instance. It is important to remove yourself from the physical danger entirely if at all possible, so that you are protected from further harm.

Perceived danger and the associated fear, anxiety and arousal, as mentioned, is a result of your trauma that gets re-ignited when exposed to reminders of the event. Your traumatic event triggered a survival response that released chemicals into your body in order to fight, flee, or freeze. Triggering this memory again releases these same chemicals, just as if you were re-experiencing the trauma.

It is important to recognize that there is *nothing* wrong with you if you are experiencing these symptoms while actual danger is no longer present. This is a perfectly normal response that your body exhibits and is designed to keep you safe in times of true danger. It also acts as a warning for you to get yourself out of harm's way quickly. We will be discussing exercises that are extremely effective in quickly helping you with this fight/flee/freeze response, but first, let us talk about what is happening when you experience these feelings.

"WHAT'S HAPPENING TO ME?"

This is one of the most common questions of trauma survivors who seek therapy, and the perfect place to begin recognizing how normal and how truly astounding and adept our bodies are at keeping us safe from danger. During the preparation for survival, you experience an "adrenaline rush." This is what happens when our bodies and brain secrete chemicals during an adrenaline rush:

- Your digestive process stops because there is no need to waste the energy required to digest when you are running for your life.
- Your immune system is depressed. Again, another waste of energy.
- Your large muscle groups are provided with energy so you can do what is necessary to survive (fight, flee or freeze); your heart rate and blood pressure increases.
- Additional energy flows to your muscles from the sugar and cholesterol that enters your blood.
- Cortisol floods your neocortex and you are no longer able to manage your emotions, think clearly or communicate effectively.

Repeated stress such as this and the accompanying decreased immunity and disruptions to your digestive system cause uncomfortable and even life threatening physical symptoms. Colds, flu, ulcers, and even cancer are associated with a compromised immune system and of course, we are all familiar with digestive issues.

You may feel that you are always in danger – that you are never truly safe and at ease, and if this is the case, you will benefit greatly by the exercises we'll discuss in a moment, but first, let's look at how our thoughts can affect our perceptions and ultimately, our behaviors.

CHALLENGING OUR THOUGHTS

Our thoughts and the conclusions that we draw have an impact on our future decisions and behaviors, especially when they have become somewhat distorted when looking through the lens of a trauma survivor.

We can arrive at very different (and incorrect) conclusions such as being unlovable, tainted, that the world is unsafe, and that people are going to hurt you. These conclusions can negatively impact how we live, and limit us from being able to enjoy activities and even the people in our lives. In short, these conclusions can keep us from our best possible future. Let's take another look at the four primary clusters of symptoms that trauma survivors experience and how they can affect our thoughts.

CHAPTER 2 TRAUMATIC SYMPTOM CLUSTERS

Four primary clusters of symptoms that affect our thoughts and behaviors occur in PTSD. Being able to recognize these symptoms and apply coping and self-soothing techniques through the exercises in the book will help you achieve our desired goal for this section: A feeling of comfort and safety. We will discuss each of these symptom clusters below and intro-duce you to a therapy client who has successfully applied the techniques you find here:

- Re-Experiencing

- Avoidance and Numbing

- Negative cognition & mood

- Hyperarousal

SYMPTOM CLUSTER 1: RE-EXPERIENCING

RECOVERY STORY
GEORGE, SURVIVED PLANE CRASH

GEORGE, A 44 YEAR-OLD MARRIED MAN WITH THREE YOUNG CHILDREN AT HOME, WAS IN A SMALL PLANE CRASH INVOLVING MULTIPLE FATALITIES. In the accident, he followed the flight attendant's instructions, particularly mindful to place the oxygen mask over his face first before helping others.

Beside George sat an elderly woman who was panicky and clearly in a high state of agitation. She was having difficulty managing to follow any instructions from the flight attendants. Once he had gotten himself settled, George turned to assist the woman with her mask and noticed her face seemed ashen and grey, her expression frozen. When the plane hit the ground, there was a sickening crash and smoke filled the interior. Although it was a terrible moment, he was able to de-plane, however, the woman beside him was unresponsive and he was not able to lift her from her seat or get her to respond by tapping and shaking her or calling her name.

Everyone was being told to leave the plane immediately but he felt an enormous amount of guilt and stress at leaving her behind in the plane, which was now filling with smoke.

Two years later, George continues to have memories that just will not go away. Whenever he hears a loud noise, sees a plane in the sky, watches a movie or TV show with a plane in it, or goes to sleep, he is flooded with the image of this woman, her panic and struggle. He feels intense shame and guilt over not having carried her out of the plane. He continues to blame himself, even though he was told after the accident that the woman had a fatal heart attack likely prior to, or at the point of, crash landing and that there would have been no benefit in risking his life to assist this woman out of the plane.

Through his work with Anna, George took the first step of developing skills to find comfort and safety once again – he learned a series of exercises to relax and ground himself in his first step in post-trauma recovery. Once he had mastered this first step, he agreed to move forward to Step 2, remembering his trauma and it was here that he made significant progress. By focusing on the difficult memory while remaining in an intentionally relaxed state (Finding Comfort), he was able to turn the corner and no longer be overwhelmed every time he had a recollection of the plane crash or any related reminders. He was able to reconnect with his family (we will discuss this in *Step 3: Beginning to Live Again!* where we will discuss reconnecting with others) - something he felt hesitant to do. He felt so guilty and ashamed that he did not feel he had a right to enjoy the love of his family or the simple pleasures of life. He was better able to reflect on the meaning of his life and the realization that as he started to recover, everyone around him began to relax and feel better as well. George realized that his guilt and suffering did not fix anything or lead to any good outcomes. He was able to begin to let go of the guilty feelings that were making life painful for himself and everyone around him. He recognized that a big step in his healing was learning to forgive himself!

RE-EXPERIENCING SYMPTOMS

Re-experiencing symptoms occur when you relive the event. Sometimes it feels almost like a movie playing in your head with a flood of memories, and yet, other times like a physical reaction in which you feel panic or extreme anxiety during a threat of intense danger even though there is none. Symptoms can begin as a result of your thoughts and feelings or triggers, which can include almost anything – a sound, a smell, another person, a color, or a song.

THE EFFECTS OF RE-EXPERIENCING

As mentioned previously, there are responses to trauma that *all* survivors experience, like feeling helpless and fearful. No matter what type of trauma endured. The intensity of Post-Trauma symptoms varies based on a number of things such as:

- Whether you were the one who was directly affected
- Whether the person, who passed away or was severely injured, was someone with whom you had a close relationship
- The length and intensity of the traumatic event
- How close you were to the traumatic event
- How much you felt in control during the event
- How quickly you received help after the event

This first set of symptoms (the re-experiencing of your trauma) can be particularly challenging and disturbing for you as you may feel like it is happening repeatedly with the same intensity of feelings, which can include:

- Recurrent and intrusive distressing recollections of the event
- Recurrent dreams (and nightmares) of the event
- Acting or feeling as if the traumatic event is recurring
- Feeling intense psychological distress at triggers or cues that resemble aspects of the event (we'll discuss triggers in a moment)
- Physiological reactions to these triggers or cues that symbolize or resemble aspects of the trauma

As you can see, George suffered from a number of these symptoms. He described the worst symptom as his inability to escape the feeling of repeatedly reliving the plane crash. Experiencing unmanageable trauma symptoms in this cluster is an early warning sign that your coping skills are no longer working effectively. This is especially true if it has been longer than one month since the incident occurred. For many trauma survivors months and even years go by before any care is provided. Finding a good outlet to work through trauma symptoms, whether through a book, self-help recording, trauma therapy or other approaches can mean the difference between years of struggle and strain versus learning, growth and recovery.

SYMPTOM CLUSTER 2: AVOIDANCE AND NUMBING

RECOVERY STORY
MARIE, CRIME SURVIVOR

MARIE, A 26 YEAR-OLD MOTHER OF TWO, WALKED INTO A BANK AS A ROBBERY WAS IN PROGRESS. She had not noticed a small group of people gathered around the manager's desk. A man with a gun in his hand was facing the manager but since his back was to Marie, she did not see the gun until it was too late. By the time she realized what was happening, he had turned around, thrust the gun in her face and had one of his accomplices lock the door. In that moment, she was trapped and shoved to the ground.

Panic washed over her. Everything moved in slow motion from her place on the ground as she turned to watch four more men jump on the teller stations, shoving long, sawed off guns into the faces of the tellers and shouting orders to empty their drawers.

Twenty minutes turned into what seemed like twenty hours to Marie. The bank robbers left the building with no one being seriously injured. However, as the robbers left, the dye packet in the moneybag that they were carrying exploded, sounding like a gunshot, a sound that stayed with her for years.

Marie was unable to enter any enclosed spaces – or any spaces from which she felt there was no opportunity for her to escape easily.

By the time she came to therapy, Marie had effectively ceased many of her social activities because, of course, most of her socializing takes place in enclosed places and they, one by one, became a source of anxiety. First small areas like elevators, restaurants, and stores became unmanageable. Then larger venues like movie theaters and stadiums became impossible to experience because she felt she might be trapped if something should happen.

Finally, these restrictions became too much for Marie to endure. The enclosed spaces were becoming a prison in her mind. She'd always recognized them as a trigger for being locked in the bank during the robbery, but she'd avoided talking about it and visiting places that reminded her of the feeling of being trapped – and thus, the perception that she had no control over what might happen next. While she was able to recognize the feelings of panic, having no other solutions that worked for her, she simply began to *avoid*.

These feelings can cause panic, anxiety, body tension and rapid, shallow breathing, so we worked on her feelings of safety – on being able to tell when she was in danger, and when she was not. Deep breathing formed a core element in her daily recovery practice. From there, we moved to a form of treatment called, Exposure Therapy, where we slowly, methodically re-introduced her to small, enclosed areas – first, in her imagination and later, by accompanying her for short trips to convenience stores and the like until, finally, she was able to go into these places by herself.

Marie came to realize that many of her fears were unfounded, as she had never experienced another trauma such as this in the 20 years since her traumatic experience in the bank. She was able to recognize that, while she would never forget the bank robbery entirely, the chance of it happening again was very slim and that the feelings of panic and anxiety could be controlled at a moment's notice. Eventually she was able to enjoy movies and sporting events again.

For more on this, we would like to invite you to view a very inspiring conversation in which Jean discusses her experience in trauma recovery – watch the interview at www.whatisptsd.com/resources. Anna speaks to Jean about her significant trauma history and the resiliency she has developed with the help of a trauma counselor. In the video, Jean talks very eloquently about emotional and physical symptoms that arise when her trauma is triggered and how a breakdown she experienced led to a breakthrough.

AVOIDANCE AND NUMBING SYMPTOMS

Avoidance symptoms are most likely to occur following a trigger. For instance, the anniversary of the trauma (the date of the incident being the triggering event) may cause you to avoid thinking or talking about it, among other behaviors.

Avoiding situations, people, places, things – even becoming engrossed in work – is almost comforting in that it allows you to detach from distressing feelings. In cases where trauma occurred at the workplace, a person might try to avoid work or any reminders of their workplace.

However, detachment is destructive over time. Eventually, in an effort to avoid, you may experience feelings of isolation from family, friends, colleagues and activities that once brought you pleasure and can lead to numbness, depression and guilt.

Even though you may try to avoid these overwhelming emotions, re-experiencing your trauma in the form of flashbacks, nightmares, intrusive thoughts or memories is very common.

THE EFFECTS OF AVOIDANCE AND NUMBING

It is not uncommon to avoid doing things that cause you anxiety, however, after a time, you may notice that your world has become smaller and smaller. You may have changed certain behaviors in order to avoid the negative emotions that certain activities bring; or perhaps turned to drugs or alcohol to manage the symptoms when they feel too strong. This second set of symptoms can be exhausting. Persistently *avoiding* something can become obsessive – it almost feels as if it would be comforting to avoid these things, but it ends up feeling quite the opposite. In addition to always being on *the lookout* for potential danger, you may also experience a loss of self-esteem as you become more isolated, limiting your experiences and even your potential.

The symptoms associated with avoidance and numbing include:

- An effort to avoid thoughts, feelings, or conversations associated with the trauma
- An effort to avoid activities, people, or places that remind you of the trauma
- The inability to recall an important aspect of the trauma
- Diminished or reduced participation in activities you once enjoyed or wanted to try
- Feelings of detachment or estrangement
- A restricted range of affect (this means the expression of your emotions)
- A sense of a foreshortened future; a feeling of dread and hopelessness

In Marie's case, she exhibited an almost exaggerated sense of hyper-vigilance and it was not until she remembered the dye packet exploding that she was able to connect the feeling with the experience. This is a good example of how her brain is wired for safety planning and reaction. In this case, the brain stored the memory of the event along with the strong emotions and physiological reactions. This means that even if Marie simply heard a glass drop and there was no actual danger, she would feel and react as if she were experiencing the moment that the dye packet exploded, something she wanted to avoid at all costs in the future because of the extreme feelings of impending doom. So, Marie's life circle got smaller and smaller so she would not feel so terrible.

It makes sense and yet, you can see that she experienced avoidance to the detriment of her social life. As we described earlier in the book, we recognize that the brain and body function in a specific way after trauma. A lot of what happens to us is really about the body and mind driving us toward safety. Unfortunately, if we continue to rehearse the fearful events in order to avoid perceived dangers, our world can become a very small place.

If you are experiencing symptoms in this cluster, you may feel as if life is passing you by as you live less and less fully. There is help, however!

SYMPTOM CLUSTER 3: NEGATIVE COGNITION & MOOD

RECOVERY STORY
MICAH, SPINAL CORD INJURY AFTER MOTORCYCLE CRASH

MICAH, IS A 32 YEAR-OLD SINGLE MAN WHO WAS ON HIS WAY HOME AFTER A LONG DAY AT WORK AT HIS IT JOB. There was a gravel truck that passed a corner just before him spilling gravel on the road. Micah hit the gravel and lost control of his motorcycle. He slid and struck a tree. Micah woke up in the hospital unable to move his legs. His fiancée ended their engagement after he was released from the hospital.

He simply could not reconcile his life before and after the crash and his mood plummeted. He blamed himself for not being able to control his motorcycle after hitting the gravel. He was plagued with negative thoughts about himself, his future and his losses as a result of the accident. He felt that he had nothing to live for anymore and that nothing could help him feel better.

Micah, was surprised that his boss wanted to have him back to work as he felt ashamed of having to arrive at the workplace in a wheelchair. He didn't want to have anyone "pity" him. He described his sense of shame and self-loathing for his physical state and admitted that he hated himself now. Prior to the accident he enjoyed sports and had a lot of friends. During his recovery he isolated himself and his negative self-talk began to crowd out any hopes he might have for the future.

His boss came to visit him at home. She reminded him that he was essentially the same guy and that he remained a valuable member of the team. Micah was surprised at the support and wondered why anyone would go out of their way for him in his current state. However, this small gesture began to crack through Micah's negative self-thoughts and depressed mood. He wondered if there might be a way to let go of the life he knew to build a new way of living that might be meaningful, but in a different way.

Micah began to embrace a new way of thinking that focused on letting go of what he knew in order to embrace what was possible now. He began to think about creating a NEW NORMAL. This opened up many doors and Micah recognized that he could still work, still socialize, still connect with others in a way that felt good to him.

NEGATIVE COGNITION & MOOD

Negative cognitions and mood symptoms occur when you are unable to recall important aspects of the trauma; hold negative beliefs or expectations about oneself, others or the world around you; blame oneself for the traumatic event; have strong feelings of fear, horror, anger, guilt and shame; disengagement from activities that were a normal part of life before the trauma; feel detached from others and struggle with experiencing any positive emotions.

THE EFFECTS OF NEGATIVE COGNITION & MOOD

What we say to ourselves can have a profound impact on our internal emotional state. In fact, for Micah he was trapped in a cycle of negative talk that resulting in feelings of self-blame, shame, self-hatred. In was no wonder that he felt unable to connect with others. Once he was able to find a way to break down the negative self-defensive wall, he started to make small steps toward reconnecting in his life and feeling better about himself.

Shame is often at the core of this negative internal self-talk and disengagement from others. Our ability to recognize our essential humanity and the reality of the frailty of human existence we can begin to embrace the good that exists today – however simple or small.

SYMPTOM CLUSTER 4: HYPERAROUSAL

RECOVERY STORY
JOHN, CAR ACCIDENT SURVIVOR

JOHN, A 52-YEAR-OLD ATTORNEY AND HIS SON, WERE SITTING AT A RED LIGHT AT AN INTERSECTION WHEN ANOTHER CAR STRUCK THEIRS. It was particularly frightening as they saw the car approach them, aiming right for John's door. He was able to move forward enough so that the other car struck the left back passenger door. John certainly would have been far more injured if he had not seen the car coming at them. The collision pushed John's son into the door, separating his rotator cuff, which subsequently required surgery. While John wasn't injured, he initially felt he was OK as he tended to his son, but as the days moved into weeks, he soon became irritable, unable to concentrate and had difficultly falling, and staying, asleep. He became more and more angry thinking of what could have happened had he not quickly reacted by moving his vehicle forward several feet before impact. Over time, his anger began to affect his work.

John successfully resolved these symptoms through treatment, recognizing that the source of his anger was a perfectly reasonable response to the trauma. He was able to integrate the loss of his concept of safety. Now he more fully appreciated the life that he had with a newfound respect for the fragility of life. His new reality included the realization that life could be taken away in a moment, but he grew to use this to allow himself to fully embrace his life experiences. He was even able to integrate this car accident into a life survival story – a story where he could celebrate his quick reaction time and the fact that both he and his son survived.

HYPERAROUSAL SYMPTOMS

Hyperarousal, also referred to as hyper-vigilance, are technical terms for symptoms such as jumpiness, feeling on edge, feeling tense or anxious, being easily startled.

These symptoms are usually constant, rather than being triggered by something else, as in the case of avoidance that we discussed earlier. As you can imagine, being constantly on edge can make you feel chronically stressed and angry. This can undermine any feelings of well-being or enjoyment in life.

Because the symptoms of hyperarousal are physiological, problems with eating, sleeping and concentrating are common.

THE EFFECTS OF HYPERAROUSAL

The anger that many trauma survivors experience in this cluster of symptoms is particularly difficult to manage as it seems to catch them off-guard – especially for those who do not often experience this emotion.

The symptoms associated with arousal include:

- Difficulty falling or staying asleep
- Angry outbursts or feelings of irritability
- Difficulty concentrating
- Hyper-vigilance
- An Exaggerated startle response

For John, the anger he felt was most difficult. He had viewed himself as a laid-back person, someone who was not easily ruffled and was able to come to accept this image of himself again following therapy. Just like training for a marathon, we will show you how to train in relaxation techniques first. We'll begin slowly and build up your abilities. For some people, years can go by before they reach out for help. If this is the case for you, do not hesitate to reach out now for help. There are many people who are there for you. Some of these people might even be in your life right now. Others might be professionals who are trained Trauma Therapists. Both of us have heard from many of our clients that when they finally started to share with others, they were surprised at the number of people have traumatic stories of their own, resulting in closer and more supportive connections.

There are many ways to find professional help. You will also find resources in this book for some ideas on how to break the discomfort of isolation and the sense that no one truly understands your struggle.

CHAPTER 3 MANAGING YOUR TRAUMATIC SYMPTOMS

As you can see from the cluster of traumatic symptoms that we have discussed earlier (re-experiencing your trauma, avoidance and numbing, and hyperarousal), managing your symptoms is paramount to your healing. Stress is a fact of life for each of us, even in the absence of trauma, and self-soothing skills that you learn here are going to help you well after you've achieved healing from your trauma.

Can you possibly find comfort, and feel *safe* again, following a traumatic event? The answer is a resounding yes! In fact, this is a *critical* first step in your healing process.

Trauma is associated with memory, and although you never lose the memory of the traumatic event that happened, over time, it can lose its intensity. Even trauma that you faced long ago may re-ignite along with the bodily sensations that went along with the original event. The term "the body has a memory" is a phrase commonly used by trauma specialists as it is recognized that the body can react as if the trauma is occurring again, when what is really occurring is a reminder of the original event.

A trigger (or a trauma reminder) can bring up the associated memory of the trauma resulting in a cascade of strong emotions, bodily sensations, rapid thoughts, and reactions. This can occur even in situations where you are perfectly safe, perhaps misleading you to believe that something is wrong with you. There is not. What you are experiencing is to be expected, but that does not make it any less confusing or difficult to go through.

In order to effectively begin your trauma recovery work, you will need to master skills to make yourself feel safe, in this moment and on demand. For this reason, it's important that you practice developing these skills, just as you would for anything that you'd like to master. Eventually, they will become second nature.

We each live within our internal worlds that are represented by our bodies, thoughts, behaviors, and emotions.   When any of these are not functioning properly, we can feel unbalanced, as if something is *not quite right.* Some trauma survivors remain in a seemingly constant state of disequilibrium (feeling out of harmony) making it important to master self-soothing and relaxation techniques.

We will discuss some essential goals that will help to manage your symptoms below and then introduce you to a number of exercises that make this possible to achieve.

GOALS FOR MANAGING YOUR SYMPTOMS

1.   Remove yourself from physical danger

2.   Gain awareness of your triggers

3.   Master self-soothing techniques

4.   Master relaxation techniques

5.   Apply your new skills daily

GOAL 1: REMOVE YOURSELF FROM DANGER

It is important that if you are in physical danger, you take steps to remove yourself if possible.   In the case of combat, war, disaster, or terrorist acts, this may be impossible in the short term, of course, and in the case of other situations such as domestic violence, it must be carefully orchestrated to ensure that you are safe from further danger.

The goal here is to plan an escape route where you can move toward a place that you can re-establish safety. We recognize that it is hard to feel safe when you are suffering from nightmares, flashbacks, and other physically and emotionally disturbing symptoms, as well as other potentially self-destructive ways of coping such as substance abuse or eating disorders.

GOAL 2: GAIN AWARENESS OF YOUR TRIGGERS

RECOVERY STORY
MAGGIE, SEXUAL ASSAULT SURVIVOR

MAGGIE, 28, WAS ON A CRUISE SHIP ON A VACATION THAT WAS SUPPOSED TO BE A CELEBRATION OF HER GRADUATION FROM UNIVERSITY. Instead, she found herself in a terrible circumstance, waking up confused, alone in an empty section of the ship, which was painted bright green, surrounded by condoms, empty bottles of alcohol and broken glass. Below, she explains her realization that months later, many of her current fearful feelings were in fact triggers to the traumatic event on the ship, and her resulting symptoms:

"A smell, a sound, even a color – I've learned that these are all considered triggers *of the trauma. A trigger is anything that reminds you of the trauma and brings up feelings and emotions. It was a smell for me as well that* triggered *the incredibly angry, hostile mood. The smell of paint and sweat lingered for months. I reacted when I smelled it without even realizing its origin. When I became more aware, through therapy, of when I was experiencing these feelings, I was able to trace it back to my trauma; I was surprised that my subconscious was so attuned and that I experienced this behavior even before I consciously become aware of it. There are ways to cope with triggers, both before they occur and during but they are terrifying. Just giving a word to it made me feel better though and feel as if I wasn't crazy."*

TRIGGERS

So, what *is* a trigger? In short, a trigger is anything that reminds you of your traumatic event. It can range from the anniversary of the event, to a song, to a scene in a movie – anything at all can serve as a trigger, causing you to relive the sensations of your original trauma.

Your symptoms, no matter what cluster they may fall in (re-experiencing, avoidance and numbing, or hyperarousal), are generally *triggered* by something else that happens, that reminds you of your trauma. Making this even more confusing and difficult to manage is that you may not even be aware that this trigger occurred, and thus, it keeps reminding you of the trauma – until you gain awareness, which we are going to help you develop!

THE IMPORTANCE OF AWARENESS

Awareness of the historical traumatic events in your life that continue to re-ignite strong reactions (or triggers) is critical in anticipating situations that cause anxiety and panic. When we have unresolved traumatic memories, they tend to steal from our present day energy and our ability to cope. These related events or reminders can trigger the earlier event resulting in feelings of distress. When we work to identify, and then resolve earlier traumas, we are able to free up our energy, extinguish the triggers, and live with a greater sense of freedom. In *Step Two*, we are going to introduce exercises that help you remember your trauma, making this awareness even more critical to your healing.

Pacing is a medical term used by cardiologists to describe regulating the timing or changing the intensity of cardiac contractions. The term, *Pacing* fits well within this section and is one that we will use for our purposes throughout this book. We can use the cardiologists' definition to help us understand what we want you to learn about starting, stopping, pausing, regulating your timing, or changing the intensity of your exposure in your trauma recovery process. It is about recognizing that you are in the control seat at all times and that if you need a break, you get to choose when and how, using the tools from this book.

We encourage you to pursue your recovery from PTSD but recognize that this needs to occur within a regulated world where you control the intensity, timing and overall pace. In fact, we find that people do better when they have the controls to start and stop.

In our view, this is a version of the child's game of Peek-a-boo where we show something and then put it away. In much the same way but with content that is of a traumatic nature, we need to be able to bring the disturbing stories from our past into view without overwhelming us and then be able to put them away again until we are ready to view them fully without being devastated by the exposure. For anyone who has shaken a pop bottle, we know that unless we let off the air pressure slowly and patiently, we would have a pop explosion. Post-Trauma emotions are much the same and we need to keep this in mind when we are working through the materials in this book.

So, you can start, slow down, or stop as needed – you are in control of this process. You may touch just the surface of your painful memories and then return to a safe or neutral state, which is incredibly empowering and affords you the knowledge that you can master your discomfort. There are a number of ways to *pace* when things become too intense, such as applying the breathing or relaxation techniques we have discussed in the Finding Comfort Exercise section. The key is to focus only on bite-size amounts of your trauma memories and to start and stop your process as needed Remember, always review and practice the *Finding Comfort* skills first prior to beginning any exercises for reviewing your traumatic history.

WHEN YOU EXPERIENCE A TRIGGER

You recall earlier that we have addressed what happens when we are faced with the perception of immediate danger and the *fight, flee, or freeze* response. Normally, the information that we need to evaluate our danger level enters the midbrain where we can determine if, in fact, the danger is real.

Danger? Both our body and mind immediately put into action a series of responses to prepare us to react, thus, helping us to get away from harm. No danger? We logically make sense of the feelings and store it. For trauma survivors, however, trauma reminders can act as triggers igniting a full trauma response that mimics the feeling of danger and evokes every bit of the associated symptoms. This makes it very difficult to correctly assess the true and immediate danger that the sound of a firecracker poses, when everything inside is reacting with a fierce intensity as if our worst trauma is happening again in this moment – when, truly, we are physically safe.

Our job, then, is to become aware of what *triggers* us, to slow down our response, to become reflective and then to evaluate whether there is actual danger in the moment. If yes, then our job is to let our smart response system get us out of danger. If no, then the job is to acknowledge the trigger and to begin self-soothing exercises in this moment so that we can gain control over our reaction and learn to manage responses.   The eventual goal, with practice, is to notice that we are reacting to something in the early stages before we have all the alarms, bells and whistles of a full trauma response ignited. At this stage, you can make the best use of the skills you are learning, apply them and retrain your body to stay calm, reflective and self-soothe out of feelings that are overwhelming.   Begin now to plant the hopeful thought that you can gain awareness of your triggers and start to lessen their intensity today.   We are going to introduce specific exercises, for gaining awareness of your triggers and managing the symptoms that ensue, in the next section, Step 2, *Remembering Your Trauma*. However, for now, it's important for you to find comfort by mastering self-soothing and relaxation skills through the exercises we'll be introducing in a few pages.

GOAL 3: MASTER SELF-SOOTHING TECHNIQUES

Your next goal in finding comfort is to master self-soothing techniques – perfect for minimizing and even entirely alleviating the physical symptoms you may feel when experiencing the symptoms of your trauma. These symptoms are related to your heart rate and breathing and can cause severe distress. We frequently hear from our clients that mastering them is particularly satisfying as it results in a feeling of healthiness and confidence in the ability to self-sooth after trauma triggers as well as in other situations.

GOAL 4: MASTER RELAXATION TECHNIQUES

Your next goal in finding comfort is to master relaxation techniques that you can call into practice at any moment and in any circumstance, whether or not it's trauma-related.

Relaxation techniques can take many forms, but it is important that we address methods for helping you feel grounded (more about this in a moment), for reducing your stress and helping to create a discipline in your daily self-soothing regimen.

Although there are many exercises to help with relaxation, we have selected several that we have found to create a good foundation and begin the process of stabilization.   More than anything else, we have found that deep breathing exercises can be extremely helpful. However, not every breathing exercise provides the same benefits or gives us the desired results. We have developed an approach that we have shared with thousands of people to good effect.   Along with breathing, we have identified several other approaches that seem to address a need to calm the body and soothe the mind. This section provides you with several of our favorites.

GOAL 5: APPLY YOUR NEW SKILLS DAILY

Whatever set of exercises from this section you find most helpful, please remember to do them daily as they lay the foundation for a stable base of comfort, a necessary ingredient in your trauma recovery. It is difficult to notice that we are stressed when it comes to a chronic condition that is depleting our well-being every day. When we experience chronic stress, we are on edge and, overall, not managing well. A healthier approach is to catch the early warning signs of stress at a low level when they are still manageable. This means that there is less of a toll on our bodies, minds and emotions (and often, the people around us as well) when we catch the feeling. It is also easier to manage stress reactions when they are less intense. It is simpler and more successful, if we can notice the early warning signs of stress and take action ourselves. Then when we are feeling out of sorts, overwhelmed and strained, it becomes obvious to us at an earlier stage of reaction as it feels quite different from the good, calm feelings we get when we are in the relaxed and stable state that we introduced in the *Finding Calm* section of this book. This is about building resiliency from states of chronic stress and finding ways to prevent a full-blown stress reaction. Learning to master *Finding Calm* exercises empowers you to gain insight, wisdom and control over what is happening to you.   When you are ready, move forward to the next chapter where you will learn to master a new set of skills for finding comfort through our specially designed exercises!

CHAPTER 4 EXERCISES FOR STEP 1: FINDING COMFORT

In *Step 1: Finding Comfort*, we have introduced you to the four major clusters of symptoms:

1) Re-experiencing

2) Avoidance and numbing

3) Negative cognition and mood; and

4) Hyperarousal

We have developed a number of exercises to help you find comfort internally and in your environment, so that you may self-soothe and relax when needed.

In each of the exercises below, we introduce you to a client who has benefited from the exercise, as well as the goals, the time-out, the materials and layout, and the instructions needed to complete the exercise.

The following is a list of exercises developed for *Step 1: Finding Comfort*:

- 3-6 Breathing
- Paced Breathing
- Self-Relaxation
- 5-4-3-2-1 Sensory Grounding & Containment
- Reflections on Self-Compassion

3 - 6 BREATHING EXERCISE

RECOVERY STORY
KATHLEEN, DEATH OF A LOVED ONE

KATHLEEN, A 34-YEAR-OLD MOTHER OF TWIN DAUGHTERS, ENTERED THERAPY WITH AN EXTREME SENSE OF FEAR AND CONCERN. She had been through therapy before and felt worried that she would have to tell her stories before she was ready. Nonetheless, she was struggling with her symptoms and felt she needed help. She summoned her courage to start again even though the feelings of panic and emotional discomfort were hard to deal with.

Kathleen described sensations of panic, shortness of breath, rapid heart rate, sweaty palms, tension in her arms, and discomfort in her stomach. Kathleen, 22 years old at the time, was with her boyfriend on a canoe trip when he died of a severe allergic reaction to a bee sting. Anaphylaxis is a potentially life-threatening allergic response to regularly harmless substances in the environment. Neither of them was prepared to treat or respond to the bee sting. Three years later, Kathleen carried a terrible sense of guilt, regret and sadness. During the interim, she developed a panic disorder and chronic PTSD.

She was very keen to understand what was happening to her and open to try a breathing exercise to gain skills to work through her symptoms. Kathleen was surprised at how much control she could gain over her breath with the *3 – 6 Breathing Exercise* below. We worked through each step and then noticed how her response changed with each deeper level of instruction. She was gaining mastery but more importantly, she now had something to practice on her own every day. This was the turning point for Kathleen who was unable to get her life back on track since her boyfriend died. Now she was feeling a sense of calm for the first time in three years – a calm that she was able to introduce on her own within her body whenever she needed it. She noted that practicing every day twice a day, with a timer (5 minutes) as she was instructed, helped to take control of her world again. She would use the 3-6 Breathing whenever she noticed her early triggers and this also kept them from erupting to a terrible panic.

We invite you to view a Breath Training video to help you with the steps of this exercise. View *"Breath Training: 3-6 Breathing: The Window Into the Nervous System" at* www.WhatIsPTSD.com.

GOAL

At the start of this exercise, it is best to focus all your attention internally and if possible, it is preferable to begin with your eyes closed. When you are focusing on your breath, sit or lie in a relaxed position where you are comfortable and will not be disrupted.   Please note that a full breath is considered an inhalation and exhalation.

MATERIALS AND LAYOUT

Pen or pencil, timer, and the form we have provided on the following pages.

TIME OUT

Do not try the *3 – 6 Breathing Exercise* if you have any respiratory problems. Instead, choose a different exercise in this section until you are safely able to work with your breath. Also, always reflect on your inner state and notice if you need a break from the exercise to find your inner calm.

PATH TO COMPLETE

1. **Noticing**

    Begin by noticing the pace, depth, and movement of the breath as you take three inhalations and exhalations (three breaths). Notice if the breath is deep, shallow, fast, slow, smooth, and rough and how it feels moving in and out of the body. After three breaths make a note of whether the breath was smooth/rough; deep into the belly/shallow into the chest; slow/fast. Capture your response below:

    _____

    _____

    _____

    _____

    _____

2. **Deepening**

    Begin by noticing that you can make the breath deeper, smoother, and slower just by focusing your attention on this task. Take three breaths again, being careful not to hold your breath at any time. When you get to the edge of a full inhalation (do not go beyond that as it will strain the body), begin to exhale, not overworking the body at any time. Bring the breath deep into the belly on the inhalation and release the breath completely on the exhalation, letting the body rest for a beat at the end of the ex-halation before inhaling again. At the end of the third exhalation stop and make a note of what it feels like to deepen, slow and smooth out the breath. Capture your response on the following page:

    _____

    _____

    _____

_____

_____

_____

3.   **Sipping**

Now you will work with a sipping breath by imagining that there is a straw in your mouth and you are inhaling through that straw very slowly and smoothly (you will need to form your lips into an "o" shape – notice you can bring the breath deep into your belly. At the edge of the inhalation begin to exhale through the nose. Do not hold or force the breath. Do this three times and make a note of what it feels like to breath in this way. Capture your response below:

_____

_____

_____

_____

_____

4.   **Counting**

In this part of the exercise, you will learn to lengthen your exhalation until it eventually becomes twice as long as the inhalation. To start with, we focus on inhaling to the count of three (you can count silently in your mind) and exhale to the count of six, pausing at the end to let your body relax. For most people, you will lengthen the exhalation over time starting with a count of three on the inhalation and reaching four, five, or six on the exhalation. The idea is not to try too hard but to let the exhalation lengthen over time with a pause to relax before taking the next breath. Continue by inhaling slowly fully and deeply into the belly to the count of three and release slowly and completely to the count of four, five or six, while staying focused on the slow full rhythm of inhalation and exhalation. Do this five times and make a note of how you feel when you are done. Capture your response below:

_____

_____

_____

_____

_____

_____

_____

PACED BREATHING EXERCISE

RECOVERY STORY
MALI, SUBWAY ATTACK

MALI IS A 57-YEAR-OLD MAN, WHO WAS ATTACKED ON A SUBWAY AFTER TRYING TO HELP A WOMAN WHOSE BOYFRIEND WAS THREATENING HER. Bystanders intervened to help but not before he was brutally struck repeatedly by his assailant. The attack left him blind in one eye, injured in his kidneys, and badly bruised. He went through intensive trauma therapy but with an upcoming court date, he feared his symptoms would return, disabling him from taking the stand. He worried how he would manage to tolerate examination and cross-examination in court. He was determined to accomplish this and saw it as a part of his recovery.

Mali worked diligently with paced breathing, practicing to speak slowly in response to questions posed in therapy. Later, when preparing for trial, his lawyer would ask questions and he would use the paced breathing exercise when responding. Inhaling and then speaking on the exhalation, he learned to manage his internal responses. This approach kept him from panicking and allowed him to say exactly what he meant knowing that he could always take the time to catch his breath and think through the impact and accuracy of his statements. He felt empowered and able to take on this final stand against his assailant.

GOAL

The *Paced Breathing Exercise* is excellent to use if you are struggling with a current issue, difficult thoughts you want to share with others, or upsetting details you need to practice speaking about (like our client, who managed to testify in court using this exercise, or our other client, who used this approach to enable her to speak at a close friend's funeral).

MATERIALS AND LAYOUT

Pen or pencil, timer, and the form we have provided below.

TIME OUT

Always reflect on your inner state and notice if you need a break from the exercise to find your inner calm.

PATH TO COMPLETE

1. Begin by identifying something that you wish to speak about but recognize the difficulty you have in sharing this story or expressing your experience or perspective. In brief, what is it you want to share?

    _____

    _____

    _____

    _____

2. What makes it difficult to express?

    _____

    _____

    _____

3. Spend 10 minutes (use a timer) to write out the event (or details to share) in as much detail as possible, as if you will be reading it to an audience.

    _____

    _____

    _____

    _____

    _____

4. After 10 minutes of writing, ask yourself, *"Is there anything else that needs to be said about the event?"* If yes, spend another 10 minutes (timed) adding more detail.

    _____

    _____

_____

_____

5.   Continue adding increments of 10 minutes until you have written all that needs to be expressed about the event.

_____

_____

_____

_____

_____

6.   Add Paced Breathing to the exercise. Practicing the *3 – 6 Breathing Exercise* creates a good foundation for paced breathing. You can use the 3 – 6 Breathing or follow the next instruction.

7.   Take a slow deep inhalation until you can feel the belly, chest and back body fill with air. Do not over work the inhalation. At the edge of a full deep inhalation, begin to exhale. On the exhalation, read your story until the exhalation is complete. Pause for a moment to let the body and mind rest.

8.   Then take another full deep breath – not rushing either the inhalation or exhalation and only speaking on the exhalation.

9.   Now work with paced breathing (or 3 – 6 Breathing) to read through the story out loud. Follow the instructions above.

10.   You can do this repeatedly until you notice a lightening of your mood or an evident lowering of your anxiety.

If you cannot achieve a lowering of anxious feelings or reduction in emotional upset, then move on to the Self-Relaxation exercise on the following page to settle yourself back down to the state of inner calm that we are all hardwired with.

SELF RELAXATION EXERCISE

RECOVERY STORY
JEREMIAH, BULLIED AS A TEEN

J EREMIAH STARTED TRAUMA THERAPY AFTER A SERIES OF EVENTS AT HIS HIGH SCHOOL. He was 18 at the time and very aware of how threatened he felt among his peers. In one situation, he was cornered while leaving the school grounds and relieved of his backpack, cell phone and money. He constantly felt alert and noticed that he was reviewing the incident over and over again. He felt exhausted from this rumination and found himself forgetting things and having a difficult time preparing for his enrollment in college, a long awaited goal. It became apparent in working with Jeremiah that he was a smart young man and just wanted to start his college program and move on with his life. His memories of the mugging and school bullying kept creeping into his mind. It was clear that Jeremiah needed help to reclaim his ability to harness all his attention and focus his mind. The exercise below was a great start for Jeremiah and a good intervention to re-train his mind to focus in a positive and calming manner.

GOAL

The *Self-Relaxation Exercise* focuses on using your internal dialogue related to the body to produce a state of very deep relaxation. While it is not hypnosis per se, you produce its effects as you master using your internal dialogue to calm and soothe your inner world. Your goal is a relaxed and restorative state.

In this exercise, you are in control of this process the entire time. However, you will need to practice it more than once to get the best long-term outcome. Remember to inhale and exhale fully throughout the exercise in order to enhance your overall experience. Your ultimate goal is a relaxed and restorative state of calm and serenity.

TIME OUT

Always reflect on your inner state and notice if you need a break from the exercise to find your inner calm.

MATERIALS AND LAYOUT

Pen or pencil, timer, and the form we have provided on the following pages.

PATH TO COMPLETE

1.   Find a relaxing place and position where you will not be disturbed. **WITH AUDIO**: Close your eyes to enhance this exercise if using the audio recording, *"Recovery Now Trauma"* (Baranowsky, 2010). See our web store, www.WhatIsPTSD.com, to purchase recording.

      WITHOUT AUDIO: Keep the book open to the Self-Relaxation Exercise page. Begin to focus and turn your attention to your breathing. Start to soften, lengthen, and deepen your breaths.

2.   Let go of any tension and tightness you feel in your body. **WITHOUT AUDIO:** Read the first sentence, close your eyes and in your mind, repeat the phrase. Open your eyes and continue to take in each instruction until you have completed the statements below:

      - *I am beginning to notice my breath*
      - *I am beginning to make the inhalation and exhalation slow and deep*
      - *As I inhale slowly and deeply I am*
        beginning to feel calm and soft
      - *My mind is feeling calm and quiet*
      - *I notice a sensation of relaxation*
      - *My right hand feels soft and light*
      - *My left hand feels soft and light*
      - *My right arm feels soft and light*
      - *My left arm feels soft and light*
      - *I notice a feeling of release in my hands, arms, shoulders and neck*
      - *My neck, jaw and forehead feel soft and light*
      - *I notice a feeling of release in my neck, jaw and forehead*
      - *My muscles feel comfortable and smooth*
      - *My right foot feels soft and light*
      - *My left foot feels soft and light*
      - *My right calf feels soft and light*

- *My left calf feels soft and light*
- *I notice a feeling of release in my feet, calves, and thighs*
- *I feel completely supported by the surface I am resting on*
- *My body releases more and more*
- *My breathing is slow and deep*
- *I feel quiet and comfortable*
- *My mind is slow and calm*
- *My body releases more and more*
- *My heartbeat is slow and steady*
- *I can feel warmth flowing from my shoulders into my hands*
- *I can feel warmth flowing from my hips into my feet*
- *I feel deeply warm and at ease*
- *My mind is still and quiet*
- *My breathing is slower and deeper*
- *I feel safe and comfortable*
- *I feel at peace*
- *My breathing is slow and deep*

6. Slowly bring your attention back to the room in which you are relaxing.

7. Begin to make tiny movements in your fingers and toes, ankles and wrists, legs and arms.

8. Slowly stretch and bring your attention more fully back into the present time and place.

    WITH AUDIO: If your eyes were closed while listening to the audio recording, open your eyes and bring your attention fully back to the present time and place.

Remember you can bring these feelings of relaxation into your regular waking day by using these focusing techniques. Repeat the exercise to teach your body to achieve a state of relaxation.

Also, remember to fully bring your awareness back to the present before attempting to use any machinery or perform any complicated tasks.

5-4-3-2-1 SENSORY GROUNDING & CONTAINMENT EXERCISE

RECOVERY STORY
SALLY, ASSAULTED AT HER WORKPLACE

SALLY WAS A 42-YEAR-OLD NURSE WORKING IN THE EMERGENCY DEPARTMENT OF AN INNER CITY HOSPITAL. She was receiving Trauma Therapy for a workplace incident in which a patient became enraged and struck out at her while she was trying to assist. She had a black eye and a broken tooth as a result. She arrived for an appointment in a state of distress, indicating that there was an irritated man on the bus who reminded her of her assailant. When she rated her stress level, it was off the chart and yet, she was able to clearly state that while she was sitting in the therapy room she was not in actual danger. She explained that that this type of reaction was pretty common for her since the workplace assault. She wondered if she was ever going to be able to be *normal* again. We worked on the technique below to give her the ability to regain her sense of calm and return to regroup herself into this place and time. She recognized that most of the time when she felt at risk, it was because the past assault was replaying in the present moment. She was ready to break this trend. The following exercise was a perfect fit for Sally.

GOAL

The *5-4-3-2-1 Sensory Grounding & Containment Exercise* assists in developing the capacity to *self-rescue* from moments where you are feeling upset and unable to settle your emotions easily.

In this exercise, you are encouraged to break your attention free from traumatic images, thoughts and feelings by, instead, focusing on and connecting with your current external surroundings through the intentional use of your senses (here and now), with the goal of reducing upsetting anxious feelings. This technique will assist you in recognizing safe environments in the present context and the value of using your sensory skills (sight, touch, smell, hearing, and even taste) to *ground* yourself to safety in your present.

You do not have to be upset in this moment to begin using this exercise because once you know the pattern you can use it at any time or place when you are upset but not in danger. Or, you can begin the exercise when you are in a safe place but still upset about a past memory or a current reminder of a past event.

TIME OUT

Always reflect on your inner state and notice if you need a break from the exercise to find your inner calm.

MATERIALS AND LAYOUT

Pen or pencil, timer, and the form we have provided below.

PATH TO COMPLETE

1.   If you are upset in the moment, begin by taking a SUD's rating (SUD's stands for Subjective Units of Distress), which is a rating from one to ten that describes a feeling of distress, where 1 = feeling calm; 5 = somewhat upset but I can handle it; and 10 = the worst feelings of distress. I feel out of control.

_____

_____

_____

_____

_____

_____

2.   Rate your current distress from one to ten. After the exercise, you can check the number again to see if there is any change in your feelings.

3.   Ensure that you are in a physically safe situation. In other words, there is no real danger present and there is nothing that you have to respond to immediately to keep yourself out of danger. If there is, then we have to start by correcting it first. If not, we can begin this exercise. Name out loud, or in your mind make a mental note of, five objects that you can see in the room you are currently in. Be certain that these are physical, and not imagined objects.

_____

_____

_____

4.   Now identify aloud, or in your mind make a mental note of, five (5) *real world* sounds that you can currently hear while sitting in the room (the

sound can be beyond the room, please be certain that you are actually able to perceive it, like the sound of an air conditioner, tapping pen, squeaking chair, your own words, etc.).

_____

_____

_____

_____

_____

_____

_____

_____

_____

5. Now identify aloud, or in your mind make a mental note of, five (5) things you can sense or feel. These are things like, your breath moving in and out of the body, the feeling of your legs supported by the chair, or the sensation of a warm breeze.

_____

_____

_____

_____

_____

_____

6. Now identify four (4) *real world* objects that you can see in the room (they may be the same or different from what you saw before). Now, identify four (4) sounds.

Now, identify four (4) things you can feel or sense.

_____

_____

_____

_____

7. Now identify three (3) *real world* objects that you can see in the room (they may be the same or different from what you saw before). Now identify three (3) sounds. Now identify, three (3) things you can feel or sense:

_____

_____

_____

_____

8. Now identify two (2) *real world* objects that you can see in the room (they may be the same or different from what you saw before). Now identify two (2) sounds. Now, identify two (2) things you can feel or sense

_____

_____

9. Now identify one (1) *real world* object that you can see in the room (this may be the same or different from what you saw before). Now identify one (1) sound.

Now, identify one (1) thing you can feel or sense.

_____

_____

_____

_____

10. Now that you have completed this exercise, ask yourself, "What has happened to my feelings of distress?" What number would best reflect your feelings of distress on the 1-10 SUD rating? Is it higher? Lower? Or the same? If you were not upset before, are you feeling even calmer now? You can use this exercise wherever and whenever you feel it will help.

_____

_____

_____

You can also choose to do this exercise while thinking of a place that you truly enjoy being in, such as a favorite park or a part of your home that is most comforting to you (as long as it is not associated with the trauma). One client chose a museum where there was an extensive rock collection. She would think of the details of the environment - the rocks that she would see, the quiet of the space and the fresh clean smell in the air. All of these features would reinforce her feelings of comfort in the moment even when she was not at the museum. This is a wonderful way to remind us of how powerful our minds are. Harnessing this power can take us out of feelings of panic and into feelings of comfort very quickly – especially with practice.

REFLECTIONS ON SELF-COMPASSION EXERCISE

RECOVERY STORY
JAKE, COMBAT SURVIVOR

JAKE WAS A 35-YEAR-OLD MILITARY MEMBER WHEN HE CAME IN FOR TRAUMA THERAPY. He received his military deployment orders 18 months earlier and, there, he faced a situation that left him feeling like there would be no good outcome. He was caught between a rock and a hard place. It seemed as if he would never be able to live with himself no matter what decision he made. While on deployment, he became aware of incidents in which children were being used as human shields, resulting in ambushes when convoys stopped for children on the road. His terrible orders were, "Do not stop, no matter what". How could he live with this moral dilemma if it should arise? He had his young children at home and the image of his children being harmed flashed in his eyes. He was horrified. This was not an order he knew he could follow, yet his troops were relying on him to get them back safely. He was always known for his courage, good character and commitment. This was shaking him to the core.

Following these orders meant the death of innocent children and not following these orders might mean serious injury and death to his platoon members. Jake was fortunate that he did not encounter a situation where he had to follow these orders in such extreme circumstances. However, he knew of others, who were forced by their situation to do things they would never choose willingly. During his deployment, he faced many disturbing events but the one that never left him was the unresolved moral dilemma of how to handle the "do not stop" order. He lost all self-respect and held himself in low self-esteem as a result of orders that he felt posed an impossible dilemma. He began to see himself as a despicable and untrustworthy person. Over time, he chose to isolate from his family and friends and he felt unworthy of their kindness. He wondered if he would always be capable of doing the most horrible deeds. His deepest work began with learning about self-compassion and the ability to build a sense of kind introspection and acceptance of the past and from this, the life in the present.

GOAL

The goal of the *Reflections On Self-Compassion Exercise* is to help plant the seed of self-kindness. It is important to develop a sense of appreciation for yourself and what you have gone through. Many people with a history of trauma also tend to be quite personally unforgiving, often carrying the burden of harsh negative self-talk. This exercise is a gentle solution to this challenging habit.

TIME OUT

Always reflect on your inner state and be aware of your need for a break from the exercise to find your inner calm.

MATERIAL AND LAYOUT

Pen or pencil, timer, and the form we have provided on the following pages.

PATH TO COMPLETE

1.   Start with a reflection of anyone (alive or no longer so) for whom you feel you can easily and fully appreciate a sense of open-hearted warmth and acceptance. Write down the names of everyone whom this applies to (person or animal).

_____

_____

_____

_____

_____

2.   Next, reflect on the center of your heart, allowing a full-bodied, warm, positive emotion to be present while you recall the person or animal. Close your eyes and hold this feeling for a few minutes as best as you can. This begins the practice of learning about compassion and as a result, increasing our ability to understand the way it expresses itself through our bodies, minds and spirit.

3.   Now repeat silently in your mind three times:
   - *May you have kindness in your life*
   - *May you have peace in your life*
   - *May you have health in your life*

4.   Write out what it feels like for you to hold this feeling of compassion toward another.

_____

_____

_____

5.   Now close your eyes and return to the heart-felt, open and warm sensation

and this time, allow yourself to shine the full feeling on yourself. Hold it as well as you can, allowing yourself to let go of any negative thoughts that surface. Again, place yourself fully within the heart-felt, open, and warm self-regard of which you are learning.

- *I embrace kindness in my life*
- *I embrace peace in my life*
- *I embrace health in my life*

6. Write out what it feels like for you to hold this feeling of compassion within yourself. If you notice that this ignites strong negative feelings at first, rest assured that it is not unusual to initially resist self-compassion and it gets easier with practice. Write those feelings down and go through the path again. The goal is to eventually work through any negative feelings, allowing them to be replaced gradually with a warm feeling of self-compassion, acknowledgment and acceptance.

_____

_____

_____

_____

7. Continue practicing daily and take note of what happens to the habit of negative self-talk.

Kristine Neff, a writer and researcher in the newly emerging field of Self-Compassion, found that those who achieve a higher degree of self-compassion tend to have a reduced risk for symptoms of depression and anxiety. Since Post-Traumatic Stress Disorder is an Anxiety Disorder, the practice of learning Self-Compassion may prove to be preventative, as well as an aid in trauma recovery. This is especially true when we struggle with self-defeating internal monologues that disable our learning and coping strategies.

CHAPTER 5 MOVING ON TO STEP TWO

Knowing when to move forward in your healing is critical, especially if you are not working with a therapist. We have established this guideline for you. However, if at any time you feel you are not ready to move forward, don't worry; there is no hurry!

Take your time to go back over the information presented in *Step One: Finding Comfort*. Remember, even if you stay with Step One for a long time, this is the most important stage of this work as it lays the foundation for all that follows in your healing. When you feel ready, ask yourself the following questions:

- *Do I feel safe? Have I removed myself from any environment in which I feel unsafe? Am I in active danger?*
- *Do I have a full understanding of the difference between danger signals and immediate danger as discussed in Chapter 1?*
- *Have I mastered the skills that allow me to take care of myself when my symptoms become overwhelming through the techniques I have learned in Chapter 2? Am I able to recognize when these skills are needed?*
- *Am I able to dip my toe in the water and allow some small memories in and out easily or do I become overwhelmed and anxious?*
- *Do I have any other areas I should work on before going on to Step 2?*

If you find that you have resolved the essential questions above, then you are ready to move on to the next step. We wish you a gentle and healing journey. Remember, there is no rush in doing this work.

The more respectful you are with your pace, timing, needs and feelings the better your experience and outcome will be. If you find you are ready for professional support at this time, then seek it out through whichever channels seem most comfortable for you (i.e., doctor, friend, family member, employee assistance program, *www.traumaline1.com*, etc.).

CHAPTER 6 DAILY HABITS FOR STEP 1: FINDING COMFORT

Even the smallest changes in our behavior can yield big results over time, but it takes consistency and persistence in order to obtain the rewards that our efforts can bring.

Even our thinking patterns, like believing we're *less than* others or as if we're continuing to be victimized, can become a habit. That's why it's very important to commit to making small changes daily. We have provided this section so you can realize a new and better outcome to each day! Build on establishing new *habits* as you master the exercises in this section and move on to the following two sections.

JUST FOR TODAY

1.   List one instance in which you gained awareness of what you were thinking in the moment.

_____

_____

_____

2.   Now list how that one moment of awareness resulted in actions, thoughts, feelings, or behaviors that are different to what you might have had previously.

_____

_____

_____

_____

3.   List one act of self-compassion that you offered or would like to offer today.

_____

_____

_____

_____

_____

_____

4.   Note a time today, or recently, that you were able to calm yourself using an exercise to find comfort (i.e., 3-6 breathing, or other approaches).

_____

_____

_____

_____

_____

_____

SECTION 3
STEP 2: REMEMBERING YOUR TRAUMA

CHAPTER 7 REMEMBERING YOUR TRAUMA

Each one of us has a narrative or a story to tell that provides us with the context of the persons we are at any given time in *our* history, based on what we have experienced and how we have survived, and how we have grown and become the person we are today. To begin remembering your trauma in preparation for telling your story, in whatever means you choose, is to give honor to your life and to begin the process of empowering yourself.

We all *hear* a voice within. Sometimes it is critical and demanding, sometimes soothing and compassionate. When we suffer a trauma, this voice can appear particularly judgmental and relentless. For instance, George, whom we met in the *Introduction*, kept blaming himself (survivor guilt) for the death of the woman sitting next to him, when he played no part in her dying.

To truly understand yourself, you must listen to your internal dialogue, for it is here where your story begins. Listen to the content with an open heart and with the intent of truly gaining insight into how your thoughts are affecting your behavior, and thus, your healing. Listen to your internal voice with empathy and compassion. Listen to your internal dialogue as you would a family member or a best friend who was sharing his or her story. Would you harshly judge or place blame on them for not acting in a certain way during a trauma? No, it's not likely that you would do that; you would provide them with compassion and empathy.

Make a commitment to provide yourself with the same level of humanity and considerations you would to those you love. In this section, we cover Trauma Memory Processing, moving into the main body of the trauma practice work that allows you to process and work through unresolved traumatic memories. Relaxation skills that you have learned and mastered thus far, as well as those we will be introducing to you in this section, are especially important as you remember your trauma.

While we both have a great deal of empathy for how very difficult it may be for you to even consider consciously remembering your trauma history, we have treated thousands of clients who have benefitted from this critical next step in healing — and seen the tremendous results.

As you work through the process of remembering your traumatic events, you may find, like most people, that your memories are not linear but rather very much out of sequence. Think of your memories as having a safety valve — you will remember salient details when it's important and beneficial to do so. You need not force your memories or feel bad if details come to you that were previously out of reach — think of it as peeling back the layers of an onion! This is a crucial step where you access your memories so you can ultimately make better sense of your trauma - an important step in lessening its intensity. In addition, with all the work you have done to prepare yourself, you are better prepared to face the trauma while employing self-soothing exercises without the same level of emotional intensity. The eventual goal and, of course, our desired outcome is that you will be able to recall the trauma without extreme emotions, bodily sensations and negative thoughts and reactions previously associated with your trauma.

Do you have a mentor, guide, or therapist? Maybe a best friend with whom you feel safe sharing your emotions? We are happy you have chosen to use this book on your recovery journey as a self-mentoring tool. So in the same vein, we feel it is possible for you to be your own guide — or Inner Wise Counsel!

Strengthening your inner core and finding your own Wise Counsel includes realizing, appreciating, and expressing your story slowly and gently at your pace. Even if it is only to yourself, so the memory loses its intensity and is integrated into your life as an event, rather than a single moment that defines you as a person. We will take a look at how the Traumatic Symptom Clusters may appear in this step and how you can alleviate their intensity as well.

CHAPTER 8 TRAUMA SYMPTOM CLUSTERS & REMEMBERING

An important part of understanding your trauma history is to look at the feelings that may be making you uncomfortable because they are holding you back from working through your story.

As in *Step 1: Finding Comfort*, we have framed the goals of this section around the four clusters of the symptoms: 1) Re-experiencing your trauma 2) Avoidance and numbing and 3) Negative Cognition and Mood and 4) Hyperarousal. During the process of remembering your trauma and telling your stories, these same symptoms may be re-ignited. Below we will address the struggle that they present and the exercises that can help you prepare for *Step 2: Remembering Your Trauma*.

SYMPTOM CLUSTER 1: RE-EXPERIENCING

RE-EXPERIENCING WHILE REMEMBERING

If you recall from *Step 1: Finding Comfort*, re-experiencing your trauma can take many forms: Intrusive thoughts, images, or perceptions, recurrent dreams or even nightmares of the event, flashbacks and physiological reactivity, causing distress. We know that these are *re-experiencing* thoughts because they are unwanted and involuntary and disrupt your quality of life when they occur.

Disturbing and intrusive thoughts can make you feel as if you'd like to escape. You may also feel as if remembering and telling your story will make it more intense and you will never be able to *forget*. It's important to recognize that we never totally forget a traumatic event, but rather our goal is to make it less intense in our lives. As with the other symptoms, you may temporarily feel, as if you are experiencing the trauma all over again. Here are some reflections to keep in mind when you feel like escaping:

- Remind yourself that you are no longer in danger in this time and place.
- Remind yourself that you have become better able to take care of yourself, through self-soothing and relaxing during these stressful times, than you were during, and immediately following, the trauma.
- Remind, and congratulate yourself, on the progress you have made thus far.
- Set your determination so your trauma has less impact on your life today.
- Learn whatever is necessary about the story, helping you to grow and make sense of the person you are today.

Ask yourself the following:

- *Did I recognize these as intrusive thoughts when they first started?*
- *Was it easier to bring myself into the present and for the symptom to pass?*
- *Was I able to reach out and speak to someone?*

SYMPTOM CLUSTER 2: AVOIDANCE AND NUMBING

AVOIDANCE AND NUMBING WHILE REMEMBERING

It is a perfectly normal reaction to want to avoid remembering, thinking, or talking about your traumatic memories. Who among us would want to bring up details that make us sad, angry, fearful, etc.?

Avoiding these memories, however, is not healthy in the end. Persistently avoiding these triggers would only serve to close your world, little by little.

Avoidance is one of the criteria for Post-Traumatic Stress Disorder as we have discussed earlier and includes avoiding not only activities, places, and people who may remind you of the trauma, but also feelings and thoughts about the trauma as well.

In time, a numbing effect takes hold of you, in such a way that you may feel detached from others, that you have avoided things that make you sad, or even that you have been unable to harbor loving feelings towards others. This is known as a restricted range of affect and can result in a seriously subdued quality of life.

Another challenge for those who avoid these sensations is the feeling of a shortened future and a life in which marriage, children, and a career are not possible for them.

SYMPTOM CLUSTER 3: NEGATIVE COGNITION & MOOD

NEGATIVE COGNITION AND MOOD WHILE REMEMBERING

The more emotion that we experienced during an event, the more acute the memories tend to be. And so it follows that if you feel negative or are in a bad mood (depressed, sad) this alone may serve to remind you of the traumatic event because the feelings are the same. This is a challenge of course; how do we remember the trauma without feeling the same negative feelings or return to the mood that we experienced. Feelings of shame are often at the core of the negative self-talk that is experienced during this symptom cluster.

SYMPTOM CLUSTER 4: HYPERAROUSAL

HYPERAROUSAL WHILE REMEMBERING

Do you feel jumpy and unable to concentrate as you sit and remember – and particularly, as you begin telling your story? Almost like you need to *tame* your racing mind?

This can make remembering your trauma and telling your story even more challenging. In addition, if you suffer from increased arousal, you may feel irritable, have outbursts of anger and an exaggerated startle response, or find it difficult to fall or stay asleep.

For many survivors, trauma is associated with the desire to escape from upsetting thoughts and memories. For anyone who has experienced a deeply disturbing event, this makes perfect sense and is a reasonable goal in trauma recovery. While simply trying to shut down our strong feelings can sometimes make it even worse, working through our history can relieve our symptoms and help us to gain insight and make sense of who we are today.

Beginning to develop an awareness of your feelings and learning to be more reflective, as a distant observer or a compassionate witness of your story, rather than as an engaged and reactive victim, can allow you to begin the process of working through your trauma history.

CHAPTER 9 TALKING ABOUT YOUR TRAUMA

Acceptance of yourself and your history is critical to preparing for *Section 3: Beginning to Live Again!*

Perspective and context is necessary for all personal growth and while we will be discussing how to nurture yourself in the upcoming section, it is important to know that your connection to your history, including your trauma, begins in *remembering* your trauma. We all have core beliefs about others and ourselves. If we are fortunate, they enrich our lives. If we are not, they can be the source of additional pain and self-recrimination and having experienced a traumatic event can greatly intensify these core beliefs.

It's important to normalize your feelings and emotions after such an abnormal circumstance as a trauma. You have already survived a situation that has shaken up your world and your courage in seeking help through this book and other resources is admirable. Building a support network, which we will address in detail in *Section 3*, is important in sharing your experience and finding compassion and empathy from those who truly understand.

THE "9/11" EFFECT

"Where were you on 9/11?"

When asked this question, many people are quick to answer – knowing exactly where they were, what they were doing, who they were with, even down to the detail of the emotions that washed over them like a wall of water – and continue to do so today, albeit, to a lesser degree unless they were personally involved. The power and dreadfulness of this experience over time has lost its intensity for some because of the influence of sharing, comforting, learning and growing. We *needed* to talk about it, as with all traumas, to process the horror together and to tell others of its effects on us and to share our grief.

Trauma carries the same personal horror for us, but often does not allow for sharing because of guilt, shame, and the self-imposed need to shoulder our grief on our own. Sometimes, we even choose not to share because we feel we must protect those in our lives. And so, we remain silent. With each bite of the tongue, with each silent oath to ourselves not to tell, we are intensifying the effect of the trauma and ensuring its intensity and influence on our lives and our future. Think of your feelings as if it were a pressure cooker. A little bit of steam must be released in order to release the pressure! If you open the pressure cooker all at once the steam rushes out burning everyone too close. This is why it is so important not only to remember but to share only a little at a time.

WHEN TALKING IS PAINFUL

There are many reasons that we do not share our stories – even those unrelated to trauma. Some of us have been discouraged since childhood with messages like, *"Big boys don't cry!"* Of course, this applies to many women as well and the message has been simply to deny your feelings in any case. For others, the ability to reach inside and access the words for the feelings - let alone identify them - is foreign. Still others may find the vulnerability and the risk of sharing make them feel extremely uncomfortable. The goal of telling your story is to construct a coherent picture of your trauma in order to lessen the intensity of those memories and to bring closure. Like every story, your trauma has a beginning, middle and an end. But for many trauma survivors, it seems as if they are stuck right in the middle – waiting for the ending. Although the danger has passed, the trauma is still felt as an ongoing event. Telling your story helps you to work through and make sense of the events, so the reminders don't continue to trigger strong responses over the course of your life.

An excellent overview of how to begin constructing and telling your story is to begin with a history of who you were *before* the trauma and what you want your life to look like after it.

CHAPTER 10 CREATING A SAFE PLACE FOR REMEMBERING

As we move toward the exercises in which you will work through trauma stories, it is important to reiterate the need for your safety and for finding comfort while on this step.

Exposing yourself to different aspects of your trauma while relaxed is crucial in experiencing your trauma differently than what you have in the past. At the same time, developing this skill allows you to significantly reduce the overwhelming emotional aspects and intensity of the trauma as well as improved ability to manage daily life with all its complicated flavors.

Remembering your trauma and telling your story need not involve reliving the experience entirely. Some emotional distress may occur but if you have mastered the self-soothing and relaxation skills you will have the tools to keep yourself safe, move through this work, and find comfort whenever necessary.

Like any skill, self-soothing and relaxation techniques take time to master, however, once you've integrated them into your behavior, you'll be able to access them when needed, even if you are dealing with something demanding or upsetting. Sometimes clients tell us that they are surprised at how much better they handle daily events that, in the past, would have been difficult for them. This is always a great sign that they are on their way to self-mastery. It's something we love to hear.

At this point, we will take the time to remind you of the need to be cautious of the signs of dissociation and its varying degrees, particularly when remembering your trauma or telling the story. If you need to, return to the brief overview of Dissociation that we covered previously. We recommend that if you are feeling unable to continue with any exercise, take a break and return to *Step 1: Finding Comfort.*

Remember, the goal of this book is to assist in your trauma recovery and this means being respectful of your pace and needs at every moment. At any point if you feel overwhelmed or need to readdress relaxation or self-soothing techniques, take the time to do it. It is essential to recognize that it is not how fast you go but how meaningful and helpful each step is for you.

CHAPTER 11 EXERCISES FOR STEP 2: REMEMBERING YOUR TRAUMA

The exercises we introduce in this integral second step of your healing help to gently remember and tell the story of your traumatic memories in a safe and effective way. As in the exercises found in *Step One: Finding Comfort*, we introduce you to a client who has benefitted from the exercise, as well as the goals, the time out, the materials and layout, and the instructions to complete the exercise. The following is a list of exercises developed for *Section 2: Remembering Your Trauma*:

- Event List Exercise
  (Please note that because this exercise is so critical to your success in remembering your trauma, we have provided you with a sample Event List based on Robert our Combat Veteran's Recovery Story, so you can see the development of his work in healing.)
- Traumagram Exercise
- Trigger List Exercise
- Layering Exercise
- Comfort In the Palms of Your Hands Exercise
- Touch Stone with Exposure Exercise
- Telling Your Story Exercise
- Developing Focus (for Re-Experiencing) Exercise
- Before and After Thinking (for Avoidance) Exercise
- Managing Your Anger In A Healthy Way (Hyperarousal) Exercise
- A Narrative Exercise: My Life Story Exercise

THE EVENT LIST EXERCISE

RECOVERY STORY
ROBERT, MILITARY VETERAN

R OBERT WAS ONLY 24 WHEN HE STARTED TREATMENT. HE HAD ALREADY RECEIVED A MEDICAL DISCHARGE FOLLOWING A PHYSICAL INJURY HE SUFFERED WHILE DEPLOYED IN AFGHANISTAN. His *Event List* will help us to understand how to prepare this type of document for ourselves. After working through Step 1, Robert was ready to identify the pivotal moments in his life that shaped him and continued to impact him every day.

Following our instructions for this exercise on the following pages, we have included Robert's Event List so that you may see how he has filled it out and use it as a guide for completing this exercise.

We will refer back to Robert as we move through the Event List Exercise and the Trigger Exercise that you will be completing in this chapter in preparation for remembering your story.

GOAL

The goal of the *Event List Exercise* is to help you to create a list of unresolved life experiences that continue to feel disturbing, upsetting, and traumatic. This lays the foundation of your work through the subsequent exercises to your ultimate goal of remembering your trauma and telling your story.

This exercise also helps you enhance your physical, emotional, and cognitive (thinking) skills and to gain awareness of, and extinguish, the events that are continually causing you anxiety.

In this exercise, you will be reviewing your life chronologically, with short, simple descriptions, starting with your birth to the present. We have provided a sample Event List below for you to review prior to filling in your own. So, let us look at *how* you can work through your memories, as well as the core beliefs that have been established as a result of your pivotal life experiences using the accompanying forms.

First, we need to remember our Subjective Units of Distress (SUD's) rating scale. You will need to rate each of the Events, based on this scale, to help you follow your progress. As mentioned earlier, SUD's describes a feeling of distress where 1 = feeling calm, 5 = some upset but I can handle it, and 10 = the worst feelings of distress; I feel out of control.

TIMEOUT

As with all the exercises presented in *"What Is PTSD?"* take the time to stop and reflect, or take a timeout, if the feelings of discomfort become too intense when working on the memories for this list. Remember that *Pacing* is one of the tools that we always encourage you to use. This helps you gauge the intensity of your feelings and the duration of exposure to your traumatic events, allowing you to feel more in control. You may choose any of the exercises practiced earlier or simply read something pleasant, call a friend, take a walk, or refocus your attention until you are able to return to the Event List Exercise.

MATERIALS AND LAYOUT

Pen or pencil, a quiet space, time, and the form provided on the following pages.

Robert's *Event List* on the following page is a good example of how to fill out the form:

ROBERT'S SAMPLE EVENT LIST

We hope that by seeing Robert's *Event List*, you will have a good idea of how this works and be inspired to take your next step with the following exercise.

Life Stage	Event List	SUD's
Early Childhood	Age 7, in the kitchen at home, Dad beat up Mom and I ran into the closet	7
Middle Childhood to Adolescent	Age 14, driving to the cottage with parents; head on collision; left sister severely injured.	8
Young Adulthood	Age 22, deployed to Afghanistan; watched a vehicle in front hit an "Improvised Explosive Devise" (IED)	10
Adulthood to Present	Age 22, first Panic Attack at the airport, after returning from Afghanistan.	8

PATH TO COMPLETE

1.   As you are reading "Path to Complete," please reference the *Event List* form that follows.

2.   Write one sentence, simple descriptions of no more than ten words. This includes a timeline (age, year, and general time frame), and a context (in the kitchen, in Afghanistan, etc.) Write just enough to recall the traumatic memory without going into great detail, as that will come later. As you can see, the Event List is broken down into age groups. However, you can start wherever you need to and you will find that you may have many events at one point of life and none in others, or only one major event while others are scattered throughout the timeline.

3.   Complete the sections as required by your age and experiences. An example of a sentence might be: *"I was 12 years old when, in front of my family home while crossing the street, I was knocked down by a boy on a skateboard."* The most important thing to keep in mind when writing out the Event List is that you DO NOT NEED ALL THE DETAILS. Only include as much as you need to recall the Event. This is a very important part of the instruction. As you can see from the example above there is not enough information there to know the whole story or even to evoke all of the worst details. It is a snapshot that captures only a slice of the story but not enough to fully ignite it.

4.   Begin your list. Be sure to remind yourself to stop in order to *pace* your exposure and intensity whenever it feels overwhelming. This *Pacing* gives you the opportunity to practice managing your symptoms with the self-soothing techniques you have learned. This helps to gain confidence in your ability to manage your symptoms.

5.   Once your list is complete, read all the memories again, this time reflecting on them by assigning them an SUD (Subjective Units of Distress

Scale) rating based on the following scale. This rating should represent your current feelings of distress as you look back on the event. Recognize that some of your memories will feel as bad as they did at the time, and others will have been resolved somewhat over time. That's okay though; every step you make in your recovery, no matter how small it seems, is a triumph! Again, the SUD rating from 1 – 10 is as follows: 1 = a calm state; 5 = discomfort but manageable; and 10 = the worst you can recall.

6.   Choose the number from one to ten that best reflects your feeling of discomfort as you recall the traumatic event. Remember, unresolved memories can ignite, making you feel as terrible as they did at the time by simply deeply reflecting on them. So, just notice how ignitable the memory is right now and this is your SUD number. Most of the ignitability is felt in your body with heart rate, breathing, body tension, fearful and anxious feelings and thoughts.

7.   Add as many memories as you wish to each section until you feel your *Event List* is complete.

EVENT LIST FORM

Life Stage	Event List	SUD's
Early Childhood		
Middle Childhood to Adolescent		
Young Adulthood		
Adulthood to Present		

THEMES

Once you have created your Event List, reflect again on all of the items on the list to identify any guiding principles, themes, or threads that weave those memories together and make them seem familiar in your life. These memories may take the form of negative beliefs (i.e., "I'm not loveable" "the world is not safe" etc.). These are the operating principles that you've established about the world around you and that influence how you act in your world. These themes have a fundamental impact on how you live your life. If everyone you encounter is viewed from a perspective of *"I am not safe"*, it will have a significant impact on how your interaction proceeds and what you get out of any potential interpersonal exchange. Having a childhood memory of being terribly mistreated can determine how you interact with a new person resulting in a sensation of remaining very stressed and chronically isolated. Learning about themes can help you challenge lifelong behavior patterns and habits. Now that you have a sense of the Events that evoke or trigger certain emotions, thoughts, and behaviors, you are better able to determine *when* you need to self-soothe.

Read through your Event List again and ask yourself, "What are my themes?"

_____

_____

_____

_____

While these events are fresh in your mind, let us introduce you to the Traumagram Exercise in the following pages. We encourage you to transfer these events as well as those of your family members' into a family Traumagram. The Traumagram will provide you with a visual representation of trauma in your family history. It may help you gain a better understanding of your family as well as the influences that shaped them and ultimately shaped you. Gaining this type of insight into not only your history but the history of your family of origin may help explain patterns of behavior and thought that reach up through the generations. This depth of personal learning can move you deeply into restructuring the life you are living so that you can move into the life that you want.

TRAUMAGRAM EXERCISE

RECOVERY STORY
CHARLIE, WORKPLACE ACCIDENT

CHARLIE, A 45-YEAR-OLD CHEF, INJURED HIS HAND WHILE WORKING AT A RESTAURANT. Although prompt medical attention saved his hand and he progressed well physically, he suffered lingering emotional effects of the accident through recurring intrusive thoughts and images – not of his actual accident, but that of an incident that happened when he was a boy. His mom was severely injured and nearly died as a result of an infection that resulted from her injury. In an effort to keep him safe in life, she overprotected Charlie, leading him to experience a sense of chronic fear – even though he was entirely safe and had healed perfectly. Charlie was experiencing an intergenerational trauma leaving him fearful and with an extreme sense of discomfort. He knew that simply *blaming* Mom was not the answer, so he wanted to gain awareness of how to move beyond this strong influence. Completing the exercise below allowed Charlie to accept that he was raised by a woman who had experienced trauma directly, impacting how he viewed life. The generational trauma that his mom passed down to him resulted in a latent vulnerability – or a secondary wound that put him at greater risk of developing PTSD. His Traumagram also allowed him to appreciate the physical and emotional injuries sustained by his mom, and other family members, and to under-stand better how trauma formed and informed them. We will continue with Charlie's Traumagram following our guidelines for the exercise on the next page, so you can see how to prepare your own.

GOAL

Our goal with the *Traumagram Exercise* is to help visually illustrate generational traumas that may be affecting your ability to heal. Often the best way to understand what is happening is through visual engagement, or a *picture*.

Genograms are used extensively in Family Systems Therapy to highlight the relationships between family members along with significant events that have taken place within the family (the *system*) that have affected behavior, sometimes over generations. A Traumagram focuses on the traumatic events that occurred throughout the generations. Our families of origin – that is, the families into which we are born or raised – can also have a big impact on what is happening to us today. We will begin with a sample of Charlie's Traumagram so you have a sense of the steps to take. We hope you will see how trauma, particularly unresolved, suffered by any family member, can impact generations to come.

In resolving your trauma, it can be very helpful to recognize that trauma can and often does go through the generations. For an interesting video on this, visit the "doctorbaran" YouTube channel in the Trauma and Biology section and select the "The Ghost in your Genes" video.

TIME OUT

Always reflect on your inner state and notice if you need a break from the exercise to find your inner calm.

MATERIALS AND LAYOUT

Pen or pencil and the form we have provided on the following pages.

CHARLIE'S SAMPLE TRAUMAGRAM EVENT LIST

Family Member	When it happened?	How they relate to family and me?	How it impacts me?
Mother	Age 8; Mother severely injured and nearly died as a result of an accident	Mom has always been supportive but is always overly cautious with me and everyone in the family. She argues a lot with my sister about this.	I see that my Mom is stressed and I try to keep her from worrying. I get angry with my sister for arguing.
Father	Age 14; became disabled as the result of a stroke during a surgical procedure; was forced to learn how to walk and talk again.	Dad is always careful and moves slowly. Everyone seems to be concerned about his health. He is a kind man.	I'm always concerned that Dad will get sick again. It scares me still.
Grandmother	1940; Grandma was in London during the bombing blitz. She still cries when she remembers it.	Mom and Grandma argue especially when Grandma gets upset. Grandma is really nice but can be difficult when she gets upset.	I tend to leave the room when Mom and Grandma argue or when she is upset. Maybe avoidance keeps me from getting close to others.
Sister	Age 22; admitted to the family that her marriage was ending	Seeing as her troubled marriage has been a source of	I feel uncertain about my choices in relationships.

	and her husband was abusive.	conflict with everyone in the family, we were all relieved when she ended it.	

PATH TO COMPLETE

1. Begin by filling out a Traumagram List for your family, based on the knowledge you have. Focus on any trauma that may have occurred during the past several generations including accidents, violence, war, health traumas, etc. Try to go back several generations if possible.

2. Similar to your *Event List*, write one sentence, simple descriptions of no more than ten words. This includes a timeline (age, year, general time frame) and a context (in the kitchen, in Afghanistan, etc.). Write just enough to document the trauma experienced by each close family member.

3. Complete the sections as required by year of occurrence or your age at the time of the event. Like in the *Event List*, you can see there is not enough information to know the whole story or even to evoke all of the worst details. Again, it is a snapshot that captures a story so we can begin to see family patterns emerge.

4. Begin your list. Be sure to remind yourself to stop in order to *Pace* your exposure and intensity whenever things feel overwhelming. This *Pacing* gives you the opportunity to practice managing your symptoms with the self-soothing techniques you have learned.   This helps you gain confidence in your ability to manage your symptoms.

5. Add as many family incidents as you wish to each section until you feel your *Family Traumagram List* is complete and we can begin your Traumagram.

6. Using the symbol system below, prepare your Traumagram showing the type of relationship each member has with each other.

On the following pages, you will see a sample of Charlie's Family Traumagram based upon the completed Traumagram List above, along with legends specific to his relationships and the incidents that helped shape his family dynamics.   The Traumagram has been simplified and does not include all family members (i.e., Aunts, Uncles, siblings, and offspring).   For your own Traumagram, we encourage you to add all the people in your family.

You will notice that in the sample, we do not have exact dates for births or deaths, etc.   That is sufficient, as a general age or timeframe is enough for this exercise. You do not need exact dates.   However, it is important to note what has occurred to each member of your family and to recognize the conflicts and behavioral patterns in a visual form as shown below.   Now you can follow the steps to create your own family Traumagram.

Charlie's Family Traumagram

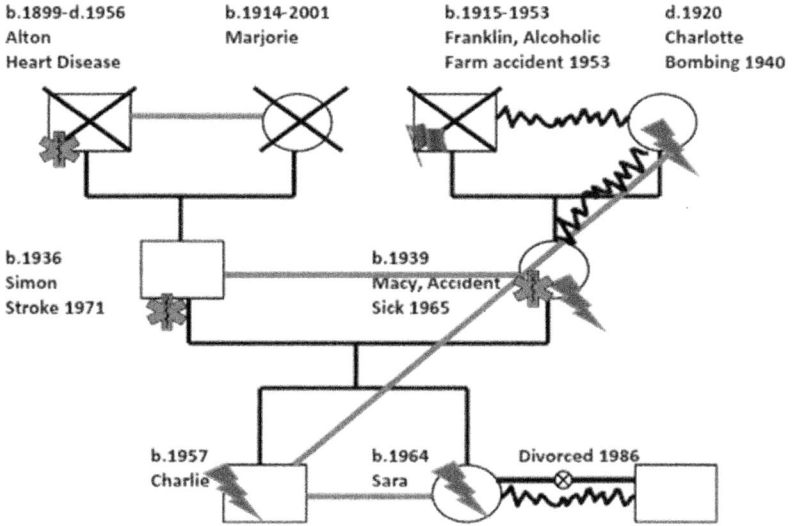

b.1899-d.1956	b.1914-2001	b.1915-1953	d.1920
Alton	Marjorie	Franklin, Alcoholic	Charlotte
Heart Disease		Farm accident 1953	Bombing 1940

b.1936		b.1939	
Simon		Macy, Accident	
Stroke 1971		Sick 1965	

b.1957		b.1964	Divorced 1986
Charlie		Sara	

Legends Used in Charlie's Family Traumagram

Traumagram Relationship & Symbol Legend

☐ ○   Male / Female

☐——○   Close / Healthy

☐〜〜○   Violent / Abuse / Troubled

☐—◇—○   Estranged / Cutoff

☒ ○   Death

Use the following symbols for your Traumagram as needed

Addictions

Ψ   Mental Health Issues

Suicide

Medical Health Problems

Traumatized

b.   Born

d.   Died

THE TRIGGER LIST EXERCISE

RECOVERY STORY
ROBERT, MILITARY VETERAN

R**OBERT, OUR YOUNG MILITARY VETERAN THAT WE LEARNED ABOUT EARLIER IN THIS BOOK, WILL AGAIN BE THE FOCUS OF OUR ATTENTION.** His story from the *Event List Exercise* helps us understand how triggers can undermine our recovery unless we can appreciate how they affect us.

After recalling his experiences, Robert recognized an important pattern in his responses after his military discharge. He was able to plug these into the *Trigger List* and this insight gave him a moment to pause before fully igniting into a severe panic reaction. His most significant awareness came when he recognized how the triggers were shaping his life.

Please refer to Robert's *Trigger List* example on the pages following our exercise guidelines.

GOAL

The goal of the *Trigger List Exercise* is to identify the triggers that lead to intensifying your symptoms. Once these emotions, thoughts, bodily sensations, and your reactions are identified, you will have greater awareness of their impact on you and be able to call into action the self-soothing and relaxation skills.

TIMEOUT

Take breaks as you feel they are needed. Always remember, it is not how fast you go but how well you are able to make sense of and integrate your learning and recovery.

MATERIALS AND LAYOUT

Pen or pencil, a quiet space, time, and the form provided on the following pages. Please feel free to download a *Trigger List Form*, and other exercise materials from our website: www.WhatIsPTSD.com/forms.

ROBERT'S SAMPLE TRIGGER LIST

EVENT	TRIGGERS
When did you feel this way?	Driving on the highway – someone cut me off; also, if I hear any loud noises; when someone raises their voice; whenever I cannot get out of a crowded place easily.
Emotions	Fear, anger, confusion, panic
Thoughts	I will never get out of here alive. These drivers are crazy.
Bodily sensations	Shortness of breath, rapid heart rate, tension in my shoulders and arms, stomach discomfort, sweating.
Reactions	Pounding on the steering wheel, swearing.

Robert's exercise reflects the places and experiences where he (our 24-year-old Military Veteran) felt most unsafe today even though he is no longer in harm's way. He described the sensation of being in traffic or hearing a loud noise as triggers that can make him feel the same way he did when he felt most at risk during his deployment. Robert might have many other places where he is easily triggered and he filled out a *Trigger List* for each of these occurrences. Mastering the ability to recognize his triggers was a big step in his recovery.

On examination, Robert could see that he was actually reacting in a way that was making him a risk on the road. He was focusing on his anger and unable to pay attention to his driving. He also realized that his past experiences were interfering with what was happening currently. Although it was true that he had encountered a driver who cut him off, he was skilled enough to manage the road. However, he was only just learning to manage his strong responses. With his increased awareness, he was determined to learn more and handle whatever came his way as well as he possibly could.

Robert can now identify when he felt most vulnerable and started to learn how to apply relaxation to help him through those moments. He was also able to start to challenge the extreme sensations of danger that erupted in him while driving or simply shopping with his girlfriend in a mall.

PATH TO COMPLETE

1.   Complete the *Triggers List* on the following page and once completed, complete the following.

2.   Identify one Trigger in your completed form:

_____

_____

_____

_____

_____

_____

3.   Reflect on the moment and write down the emotions, thoughts, bodily sensations, and reactions that go along with this memory.

_____

_____

_____

_____

_____

_____

4.   Now reflect on events or situations that evoke the same response. These are your Triggers; recognizing them can be very freeing as you can trace these back to the original traumatic event(s) and begin to ask yourself whether this reaction is more about the past than the present. This is another way to challenge whether you are currently safe or you are responding automatically to something that reminded you of a truly dangerous time.

_____

_____

_____

_____

_____

_____

THE TRIGGERS LIST EXERCISE

EVENT	TRIGGERS
When did you feel this way?	
Emotions	
Thoughts	
Bodily Sensations	
Reactions	

LAYERING EXERCISE

RECOVERY STORY
SABRINA, SUFFERED FROM MULTIPLE TRAUMAS

SABRINA'S EVENTS LIST HAD SO MANY ITEMS SHE WASN'T SURE IF THIS WAS "NORMAL" AND ASKED ABOUT IT. Having worked with many individuals, who have experienced complex trauma histories with multiple events, I was able to reassure her that it was unfortunate but was the case for many people. Sabrina was 27 when she started Trauma Therapy and had recently started her training to become a flight attendant. She was thrilled about her new career but remained concerned about her trauma history interfering with her goals. She had experienced intrusive memories, disturbing trigger responses and feelings of panic. She felt quite positive about the recent changes she had made in her life and she felt encouraged with the idea of feeling better overall. Sabrina had 41 items on her Events List that ranged from being thrown in the lake by a drunken Uncle to "teach [her] to swim"; being sexually assaulted by a neighbor; being held up by gunpoint; and the list went on. Sabrina was quite a remarkable young woman who made a commitment to herself to make sense of her life and work through what had happened.

In her Events List, there were certain items that stood out for her that made her recognize they were at the heart of her feelings of vulnerability and most likely to intrude in her thoughts. When asked, "Which event would you choose to resolve that would give you the greatest sense of relief if it were no longer troubling you?" she did not hesitate when given this choice. Immediately she said, "I was 16 [when] I opened the door to the family home and was confronted with a neighbor who held a gun and pushed his way into the house. He was screaming that the Police were next door searching for him and he didn't want to be found." She explained that "He held [them] hostage for 24 very scary hours, while he came down from the crack cocaine he was using. Eventually, he gave himself up but while he was in the house he terrorized everyone." She went on to say that "[her] Grandparents were

with [them] and so was [her] baby sister. [She] was afraid for everyone's safety."
This was Sabrina's #10 - her worst memory. The one that bothered her more than
anything else and she said it was the memory she wanted to work on.

She had very good results with the *3 – 6 Breathing Exercise* and we chose to use this
as a foundation for the Layering Exercise that follows below. This was the exercise
we used to work through and resolve her traumatic memory.

GOAL

The goal of the *Layering Exercise* is to help you draw on techniques that you have
already begun to master in *Section One: Finding Comfort* and earlier in this section
as well.

Deep breathing is a central component to this exercise and so, we recommend that
you become familiar with and master the use of a deep breathing method prior to
using this exercise. See *Step 1: Finding Comfort*, if you need to review breathing
exercises.

Layering can be used whenever you have a heightened sense of distress over a
recent event. Once you are comfortable with how Layering works, you can use it to
help you resolve a traumatic memory. We suggest that you start with a memory
that is more manageable and then over time, once you become skilled at Layering,
you can use this approach as a Mastery technique for managing feelings of distress
related to a specific traumatic memory or any current event. Layering is a self-
mastery exercise that allows you to focus on a disturbing memory, then on self-
soothing and alternating between both until you feel more relaxed when recalling
the details of an upsetting memory.

Use this exercise to enhance your coping skills when feeling anxious or to simply
relax and restore yourself. Remembering your trauma and telling your story can
bring up old feelings and make you feel as if you are experiencing the trauma – but
above all, keep yourself safe.

TIME OUT

Don't begin this Layering Exercise if you are actively dissociating, if you begin to dissociate during the exercise or if you have a respiratory ailment. If you are unable to use Layering, this exercise can be substituted for the *Comfort in the Palms of Your Hands Exercise* that we will be describing in a moment.

MATERIALS AND LAYOUT

Paper, pencil and the form provided on the following pages. Additional *Layering - Charting* forms can be downloaded from our website at: www.WhatIsPTSD.com/forms.

PATH TO COMPLETE

Complete the *Layering Exercise Form* on the following pages using the instructions below as a guideline:

1.   Identify the source of discomfort or disturbing memory. Rate it from one to ten on your SUD's scale. As mentioned earlier, SUD's describes a feeling of distress where 1 = feeling calm; 5 = some upset but I can handle it; and 10 = the worst feelings of distress; I feel out of control.

2.   Now begin to focus on your breathing using one of the breath exercises practiced earlier. Alternatively, focus on the center of the palms of your hands, picture a warm glowing ball, soothing and softening in your palms. Imagine the warmth radiating from the palms.

3.   If using breathing as your self-soothe skill, practice with five deep inhalations and exhalations throughout. Review the breathing exercise described earlier, if needed.

4.   Begin by either writing or speaking aloud what has occurred or what keeps this memory disturbing for you. Keep the initial description as succinct as possible to begin with.   Add more details as you become more comfortable with the content. Maintain calm without losing control of your breath or comfort in the palms of your hands.

5.   As you begin describing the event, remain aware of your breathing or comfort in the palms of your hands. Stop whenever you recognize a noteworthy change in breathing or loss of comfort.

6.   Now focus inwardly and begin five deep inhalations and exhalations as you learned earlier, or focus on increasing comfort in the palms of your hands. After the fifth exhalation, focus outwardly again.

7.   Take a SUD's rating based on how you feel now. If the SUD's is higher than five, take five more deep breaths. If five or lower, begin to describe more about the event that has been causing you discomfort.

8.   Continue with this process until the SUD's rating has been consistently reduced to below five while describing the entire event.

LAYERING EXERCISE FORM

ID Target Event   SUD's

Emotional Reaction

Thought

What is it that makes this event so upsetting?

Outcome

What happened?

Deep Breathing (5 times or comfort in one part)

Target Event (further description)

Deep Breathing (5 times or comfort in one part)

Cognition

What thoughts go along with this experience?

Deep Breathing (5 times or comfort in one part)

Emotion

What feelings do you have about this event?

Deep Breathing (5 times or comfort in one part)

Bodily Sensation

What feelings of discomfort do you have in your body?

Deep Breathing (5 times or comfort in one part)

Emotion

What feelings do you have about this event?

Deep Breathing (5 times or comfort in one part)

Emotion

What feelings do you have about this event?

Deep Breathing (5 times or comfort in one part)

Continue working with the stages of this exercise until your SUD's rating is five (5) or lower. If you cannot reduce your response to five or below using the Layering approach, return to one of the other exercises from *Finding Comfort* to achieve this sense of inner peace.

COMFORT IN THE PALMS OF YOUR HANDS EXERCISE

RECOVERY STORY
BARB, ACCIDENTAL DEATH OF HER MOTHER

BARB, A 34 YEAR-OLD MOTHER OF FOUR, EXPERIENCED A TRAUMA AT THE AGE OF SEVEN WHEN SHE FOUND HER MOTHER LYING AT THE BOTTOM OF THE BASEMENT STAIRS. She had fallen on her way to do the laundry and had died from her injuries at some time during the day. Barb grieved terribly and suffered from tremendous guilt, continuing to hold herself at fault for having stopped off at a friend's house after school. She had convinced herself that had she come home earlier, she would have been there to help her mom in time. Barb found out as an adult that an autopsy had shown that her mother had passed away, as best could be determined, within a three hour window in the morning – there was nothing she could have done, however, she suffered tremendous survivor guilt for years.

Barb started grief counseling in her early 20s, however, had become busy with her family and never returned. The recent death of a very close friend triggered the emotions she suffered from the death of her mom. Some days for Barb were better than others and while her previous counselor diagnosed her with PTSD, she never felt as if she fully resolved these issues. She found it difficult to trust the therapist she was seeing and had difficulty forming any long-term relationships, feeling afraid that they would leave her as her Mother had. As she neared the age that her mom died, and with two children under the age of seven, Barb began experiencing extreme anxiety that led to panic attacks and mild dissociation with accompanying physical symptoms including shortness of breath.

In utilizing this exercise, Barb was able to achieve a state of relaxation and calm, to ground her mind and to reduce dissociative events when she recognized an impending panic attack.

GOAL

The *Comfort In the Palms of Your Hands Exercise* helps you focus on achieving a state of calm in the center of your palms – and excellent substitute for deep breathing. This exercise follows the same formula as Layering. This is a good alternative for individuals who find it difficult to gain comfort using their breath.

TIME OUT

Always reflect on your inner state and notice if you need a break from the exercise to find your inner calm.

MATERIALS AND LAYOUT

Pen or pencil and the form on the following pages.

PATH TO COMPLETE

	Target Event	SUD's
1.	Identify the Event that you want to work on in this exercise. Before you begin, rate the memory using the SUD scale and return to this rating before you finish the exercise. An SUD describes a feeling of distress where 1 = feeling calm; 5 = some upset but I can handle it; and 10 = the worst feelings of distress, I feel out of control.	
2.	Focus on the center of the palms of your hands.	
3.	Imagine a warm sun beaming into the center of the palms of your upturned hands.	
4.	Allow yourself to sense a feeling of warmth and relaxation, soothing and smoothing out the center of the palms of your hands creating a feeling of release that radiates throughout your hands to your fingertips and up your arms into your shoulders and neck. Imagine the warmth spreading and easing any discomfort you may be feeling. Continue to monitor the comfort in your hands. Whenever you lose comfort, this is a signal to take a break and find comfort again. Once you are able to achieve a sense of *Comfort in the Palms of your Hands*, follow the steps from the Layering exercise above substituting Comfort in your Palms for Breathing.	

TOUCH STONE WITH EXPOSURE EXERCISE

RECOVERY STORY
STEVE, ASSAULT & RESULTING HEALTH TRAUMA

STEVE SUFFERED AN ASSAULT AT A RESTAURANT WHEN COMING TO THE AID OF A SERVER BEING CONFRONTED BY CUSTOMER. It had been seven years since the assault and he thought he had put the incident behind him, but a recent medical diagnosis of Multiple Sclerosis left him fearful for his, and his family's, future. Asked by his physicians early in the diagnosis phase whether he had suffered any head trauma, his thoughts immediately turned to the injuries he received during the assault. While he never regretted coming to the aid of a stranger, and in fact, acted without the thought of his safety, he was now questioning whether his actions on that day led to a more unfortunate outcome than he previously realized. Perhaps it had a more serious impact than he originally thought on his physical health. His mind was racing with these thoughts and they seemed to be the source of his troubled sleep as well as memories of being struck in the restaurant along with feelings of fear. In fact, he found himself acting as if it had happened yesterday.

This exercise was particularly helpful for Steve because it allowed him to use both the power of his mind and body to refocus on the positive, as well as engage him in a process that works through his troubled past. He was also able to come to terms with his diagnosis and find ways to feel more settled in his body and mind. He knew that it was important to work through his struggles so that they would not worsen his health condition.

GOAL

The *Touchstone with Exposure Exercise* is a process designed to encourage feelings of comfort, security, and safety and can be accessed at any time and any place once it is well established. The exposure part of this exercise allows you to focus on the safety established in *Section One: Finding Comfort*, while working through an unresolved memory.

So what is a Touch Stone? A Touch Stone is a way of physically reminding us to focus and rehearse a certain state of being. In the case of this exercise, the state will be a reminder of comfort and safety (or similarly reassuring feelings). We use a simple physical reminder or Touch Stone (i.e., small stone or other object) like a pebble that you can hold comfortably in your hand. You could also use a Touch Stone like a special ring, positive saying, favorite picture or even your or thumb and finger pressed in the OK symbol. Whatever you like that is easy to access is a good Touch Stone or physical reminder of the desired state.

For the purpose of this exercise, we suggest a Touch Stone that is a found rock or object that you can hold easily within your dominant hand (the hand you write with). Practice holding the Touch Stone in your dominant hand with a light, but consistent pressure with your eyes closed, so you will experience how it feels before you start the exercise. Throughout the following exercise, you will need to read the instructions and then take a few moments of reflection. Closing your eyes throughout for reflection will help keep you connected with your experience.

TIME OUT

Do not use this exercise if you are actively dissociating. As always, reflect on your inner state and notice if you need a break from the exercise to find your inner calm.

MATERIALS AND LAYOUT

Pen or pencil, Touch Stone (found rock or object that fits comfortably in your hand) a quiet space, time, and the form provided on the following pages.

PATH TO COMPLETE

Part 1: Positive Inner State

1. Identify a time/state when you felt a sense of inner calm, security, pleasure or contentment (i.e., at the beach on a sunny day):

    _____

    _____

    _____

    _____

    _____

2. Add details of the memory of this calm and safe state when you felt the best (i.e., at the cottage, quietly sitting on a chair with a book, hearing the crackle of the fireplace warming the room):

    _____

    _____

    _____

    _____

    _____

3. Close your eyes and re-experience this positive moment (10 – 15 seconds).

Behavior

4. Close your eyes and imagine you are watching a videotape of this experience.

5. Make a note of images that are played in your own mind. What did you see yourself doing?

    _____

_____

_____

_____

6. What was the look on your face in this calm and safe moment? Make a note of this below:

_____

_____

_____

_____

Thoughts

7. Reflect again on this calm and safe moment and replay it in your mind. This time, notice the positive inner thoughts that go along with such moment.

8. Note below the positive internal thoughts that go along with this calm and safe moment.

_____

_____

_____

Body Feelings

9. Return to the positive memory and, again, rehearse the best moment. Notice the feelings in your body that go along with this calm and safe memory. Make a note of what you feel in your body. What sensations go along with a positive memory?

_____

_____

_____

_____

_____

_____

Setting the Touch Stone

10.   Return to the positive memory, recalling all the images, thoughts, feelings and bodily sensations that go along with it. Really let yourself experience it as deeply as possible.

11.   Again, recall the positive memory of what you were doing at the time, your emotions, thoughts and bodily sensations. Let yourself be fully immersed in this memory and then write all additional details that you notice now:

_____

_____

_____

_____

_____

_____

12.   Read through your description above, close your eyes and allow yourself to capture as much of this experience as you can, as if you were reliving it in this moment.

Connect the Touch Stone to the Positive Memory

13   When the positive memory and the sensations that go along with it feel as good as possible, gently squeeze the Touch Stone in your dominant hand for five seconds, putting all the positive, calm and safe feelings into the gentle but firm squeeze.

14. Bring your attention back to the present moment and the room you are sitting in.

15. Test the Touch Stone by holding it firmly, trying to recall as much of the Positive Memory as you can. Notice how much of the memory you can restore by focusing on the Touch Stone.

Part II: Exposure

16. Identify an item from your Event List or Triggers that you want to work on in this exercise. Reflect on the experience, your feelings, thoughts, and bodily sensations at the time of the incident. Notice how ignitable the memory is right now. Rate it from 1-10 (1 is not at all disturbing and 10 is the worst feeling). SUD's = _____

17. Squeeze the Touch Stone in your hand for five seconds, putting all the positive emotions, thoughts and sensations associated with the resource state you have identified earlier into the squeeze.

18. Imagine yourself being fully present in your positive state. Feel it, see it, live it. Then relax your hand holding the Touch Stone.

19. Return your attention to the memory from the Event or Trigger list. Reflect again on the thoughts, sensations, behaviors, emotions associated with the unresolved memory. Notice the intensity of the memory and the feelings that go along with it.

20. Now, again, squeeze the Touch Stone in your hand for five seconds, putting all the positive emotions, thoughts and sensations associated with the resource state you have identified earlier into the squeeze.

21. Imagine yourself being fully present in your positive state. Feel it, see it, live it. Then relax your hand.

22. Test your SUD's level now as you reflect on the Trigger or Event. Write out the SUD's level here: _____

28.   Return to the top of #16 of this exercise and follow through again until the SUD's rating is a five or less and the memory feels more integrated. Note that a lightening of emotions and increased body relaxation is a good indicator to end the exercise. If the memory does not resolve to lower than an SUD's of 5, then return to the *Step One: Finding Comfort Exercises* until you experience a greater sense of relaxation.

_____

_____

_____

_____

_____

_____

TELLING YOUR STORY EXERCISE

RECOVERY STORY
MICHELLE, ABUSIVE RELATIONSHIP

MICHELLE SPENT TWO MONTHS IN A BATTERED WOMAN'S SHELTER WITH HER TWO CHILDREN AGED EIGHT AND TWELVE. She went back to her husband and the violence worsened. Just when she thought it could not get worse, she struck back while they were standing on the porch of their home. He slipped and fell, hit his head and went into a coma. She called 911 and explained the story. Police and ambulance arrived at the home. They took him to the hospital and she was taken to the police station while a family member came to stay with the children. She was shocked to be charged with assault when her husband remained in hospital due to his injuries after the incident. Michelle's story was deeply troubling to her.

She felt ashamed for staying so long in an abusive relationship, but confused and disturbed at the result of their final altercation. No matter what she felt before the final incident, he was the father of her children and now he was injured. She simply could not come to terms with how things happened so quickly and how it was possible that he was in a coma. Michelle had a big complicated story to work through with the history that came before. An approach that allowed for deeper storytelling and time to work through the events was a good option for her. The next exercise led to a good result for Michelle.

GOAL

The *Telling Your Story Exercise* incorporates exposure to a difficult memory and our thoughts. The goal of this exercise is to confront and challenge beliefs and thoughts that may be a result of a trauma. This exercise is especially helpful with feelings of survivor guilt and self-blame. In addition, it can help you face strongly held, distorted beliefs whether they are about trust, power, control, self–esteem, or intimacy that are no longer working at this point in your life. Continue to work through the stages of the exercise until you begin to notice a lessening of feelings of being *stuck* so you can begin to move ahead in your recovery.

TIME OUT

Do not use this exercise if you feel overly confused or are overly stressed, actively dissociated, or if you find yourself dissociating during the exercise. Always reflect on your inner state and notice if you need a break from the exercise to find your inner calm.

MATERIALS AND LAYOUT

Pen or pencil, timer, and the form we have provided on the following pages.

PATH TO COMPLETE

1.   Identify an unresolved memory, concern or situation. Use the SUDs rating scale (1-10). Select the number that reflects your feelings of distress regarding the memory right now. SUD rating = ___

_____

_____

_____

_____

_____

_____

2.   For one minute, remain in quiet reflection, letting your thoughts run with no judgment on the content. This should be a timed minute, ending when the buzzer goes off.

3.   Now set the timer for five minutes. Use this time to write out the details of the thoughts that surfaced during your one minute reflection, allowing yourself to do this without judgment or suppression so you can capture everything you recall (add paper if needed) [Stop at the end of five minutes].

_____

_____

_____

_____

_____

_____

4.   Repeat items 2 and 3 until your SUD's ratings are a five or less.

5.   Remember to work with exercises to relax and lower stress whenever needed. Be deliberate about this and always notice changes in your emotional and physical state.

DEVELOPING FOCUS EXERCISE

RECOVERY STORY
SIMONE, CAR ACCIDENT SURVIVOR

SIMONE WAS THE LONE SURVIVOR IN A CAR ACCIDENT THAT TOOK THE LIVES OF TWO OTHER PEOPLE; STRANGERS TO HER IN ANOTHER CAR. After a relatively short hospital stay, she found that, although she looked well, she suffered terribly from recurrent thoughts about the accident and the people who lost their lives. Simone was unable to focus on anything in her life. Prior to the accident, she held a job and was attending school, but after being released from the hospital, she felt everything slipping away. She was laid off and had to quit school due to her lack of income. Even finding a new job had become nearly impossible as she spent most days surfing the Internet, mindlessly moving from one thing to the next, and revisiting news accounts of the accident. Her lack of focus due to these intrusive thoughts threatened to derail all her life goals. Because of the severity of the accident, Simone found that the images and thoughts simply would not leave. She had never experienced anything as traumatic as this and was at a loss as to how to release her mind from this constant imagery. Through the exercise below, she was able to comprehend the significance of exposure to triggers and subsequent unwanted intrusive images of the accident. Her habit of visiting websites that contained photos of the accident had the undesired effect of reigniting her distress without any way of comfortably working through the event. Once she was able to break this connection, she began experiencing fewer intrusive thoughts and an increased ability to focus on getting her life back on track.

GOAL

The goal of the *Developing Focus Exercise* is to enhance your focus and trauma processing skills while working through the effects of the first cluster of trauma symptoms – re-experiencing. Because intrusive thoughts, dreams, perceptions, etc.

are an issue in this cluster of symptoms, developing the ability to focus can extend into other areas of your daily life, and can help there as well!

TIME OUT

Always reflect on your inner state and notice if you need a break from the exercise to find your inner calm.

MATERIALS AND LAYOUT

Pen or pencil and the form we have provided on the following pages.

PATH TO COMPLETE

1.   The next time you have an intrusive thought, take several breaths and remind yourself that you are no longer in danger. You are in the here-and-now. You are safe and you are in control. What words would you say to a close friend to reassure them at a time like this? Write out those words below:

_____

_____

_____

_____

_____

_____

2.   Remind yourself that you are able to take care of yourself and that you recognize this as an intrusive thought caused by a trigger. Remember, trigger reactions might occur to something you have experienced in the moment, earlier in the day or even something you saw last night on TV. A trigger does not have to be close in time to your reaction to form the connection. What was this trigger?

_____

_____

_____

_____

_____

_____

3.   Congratulate yourself on the progress you are making in being able to recognize the link between the trigger and the subsequent intrusive thought. Write the connection between the two here (i.e., I saw a movie last night where a child was hit and it reminded me of a time when I was vulnerable as a child):

_____

_____

_____

_____

_____

_____

End this section by reading through your thoughts from item #1 above.

BEFORE & AFTER THINKING EXERCISE

RECOVERY STORY
ANTHONY, 9/11 SURVIVOR

ANTHONY STILL GETS UP EACH DAY, AND TAKES THE TRAIN TO MANHATTAN – BUT FOR HIM, EVERY SUNNY DAY IS A REMINDER OF THE DAY WHEN HE LOST A NUMBER OF FRIENDS AND COLLEAGUES. Although September 11th comes each year, for Anthony, time has stopped in many respects. Not scheduled to come into work this day, Anthony had received a last minute call from a friend who asked him to take the friend's shift – and he shortly found himself fully engulfed in a trauma that he is unable to accept or move past. His *before* and *after* thinking, a cognitive system in which one strongly, and often wrongly, differentiates how life worked before and after the incident, doesn't even occur on a conscious level, but rather it is so deeply ingrained as a part of his thinking that, as he explains it, it simply "is." The *Before and After Thinking Exercise* helped Anthony realize that many of his same strengths, his personality traits and even his weaknesses were much the same, both before and after the event that he survived. He still suffered the same frustrations as before the event but his real issue was in recovering from them as quickly as he would have prior to it. He determined that he lacked his old resolve – to a large part, it was because he was continuing to question why he had survived and so many of his friends had not. This constant questioning was affecting his ability to move past the trauma, so that he could begin living life again. Realizing that this may be a question that would never be answered to his satisfaction, he resolved to at least live life again on his terms. In addition, he was determined to complete the exercise for, at the heart of the matter, he was a New Yorker.

This was an integral part of his pride and his history and he felt that, as a New Yorker, he had a steely resolve and a survivor instinct that had been buried for far too long – this too was being stolen from him along with his friends.   Through this narrative exercise of telling his story, he realized that the same strengths that he had relied on his entire life would serve him well right now if he was determined to apply them. Just as important, though, was his realization that he had avoided thinking about the attack in order to appear strong and in charge – a coping mechanism that was no longer working for him and one that he resolved to change. He joined a support group and was surprised at the number of people still attending years after the event. He had thought he was alone in his grief and simply knowing he had a support system was a tremendous help.

GOAL

The goal of the *Before & After Thinking Exercise* is to help you break through the barriers that may be keeping you from remembering, and telling, your story. Avoiding and numbing in the second cluster of traumatic symptoms is very common among people who place their history in *before* and *after* boxes. The exercise below helps you to integrate and blur the line between the two so you can ultimately let the trauma become part of your history, a distant memory, rather than the event that ultimately and entirely defines your life.

TIME OUT

Always reflect on your inner state and notice if you need a break from the exercise to find your inner calm.

MATERIALS AND LAYOUT

Pen or pencil, timer, and the form we have provided on the following pages.

PATH TO COMPLETE

1. Describe what you were doing before your traumatic event, i.e., were you working? Going to school? Married or dating?

    _____

    _____

    _____

2. Now describe yourself after your traumatic event. How did you change? Did you return to work or school? Did you have the same relationships?

    _____

    _____

    _____

    _____

3. Describe your moods before your traumatic event. Were you suffering from any depression or anxiety, etc.? What was happening for you emotionally?

    _____

    _____

    _____

    _____

    _____

    _____

4. Now describe your moods following your traumatic event:

    _____

    _____

    _____

    _____

    _____

    _____

    _____

    _____

5. What were you like as a teenager (or younger if you are a teen now)?

    _____

    _____

    _____

    _____

    _____

    _____

6. What personality trait did you like about yourself as a younger person that you would like to reclaim now?

    _____

    _____

    _____

    _____

    _____

    _____

7.   Do you still have the personality trait? If not, why? Do you feel that the trauma has taken it from you?

_____

_____

_____

_____

_____

_____

8.   What sort of things made you happy, angry, sad, or frustrated before your traumatic event?

_____

_____

_____

_____

_____

_____

9.   After the trauma, what makes you happy, angry, sad, or frustrated now?

_____

_____

_____

_____

_____

_____

10.   How easy is it for you to *recover* from these feelings? Is this different from before your traumatic event?

_____

_____

_____

_____

_____

_____

11.   Do you feel there is something that your trauma has *taught* you? What is it and how can it help with problems you may encounter now and in the future?

_____

_____

_____

_____

_____

_____

MANAGING YOUR ANGER EXERCISE

AMANDA COULD ALMOST SEE RED WHEN SHE BECAME ANGRY. Her father died when she was in high school and she began to gain a significant amount of weight. Her classmates cruelly taunted her for her weight gain leaving her feeling humiliated and enraged. They seemed to show no sympathy for her loss or recognition of the impact of their torment. As she aged, the injustice just hurt more. Her grief, along with the bullying, simply felt too much to endure. As an adult, these feelings of rage only seemed to intensify when faced with both everyday slights that we all endure, as well as real negative behavior from an overbearing, domineering boss. These bullying tendencies from her boss reminded her of the taunts that she received daily – and of her grief and loss.

Amanda knew that managing her anger needed to be her top priority. She noticed that the storytelling exercises in this chapter began to help her change her perspective and move towards resolving her past; first, in regards to the loss of her father, then, of her previously healthy self, and finally, of her sense of self-esteem. Once she was able to connect this bullying behavior from her boss to her past trauma, she was able to put her anger into perspective. She eventually moved on from that job and began to focus on behavioral changes to achieve her desired healthy eating and exercise programs.

GOAL

The *Managing Your Anger Exercise* helps you to cope with the effects of the third cluster of trauma symptoms, hyperarousal, and is effective when you are feeling angry or irritable.

TIME OUT

Always reflect on your inner state and notice if you need a break from the exercise to find your inner calm.

MATERIALS AND LAYOUT

Pen or pencil and the form we have provided on the following pages.

PATH TO COMPLETE

1. Make use of simple relaxation techniques, such as the *3 – 6 Breathing Exercise* that we introduced in *Step 1: Finding Comfort,* to calm yourself as you feel your anger building.

2. Try to gain awareness of what happens within your body when you start feeling angry. There are clues if we learn to read them; for instance, does your breathing become shallower? Do you start to clench your fists? Does your heart start to pound? Do you get a stomachache? Headache? Tense muscles? Anger is a normal and natural response. However, physical symptoms can signal that your anger is becoming out of control and no longer something you can learn from. List five or more signs that anger is rising inside of you. These are your early warning signals. Make a note of them below:

_____

_____

_____

_____

_____

3. Identify several anger management techniques that you will use next time you begin to feel angry, so you have them at hand. Techniques that are helpful include:
    - Counting to ten
    - Distracting yourself with something you enjoy doing
    - Reaching out to a friend
    - Writing about your anger on a piece of paper and committing to work through it later
    - One of our favorites and a great technique: Exercise!

Identify what has worked for you in the past in releasing anger or getting through an angry moment. Have you been able to use Step 1 exercises to help you when you are feeling overwhelmed and emotional? Any of these can be used when you are feeling angry.   List whatever has worked for you in dealing with anger below. Keep this list handy and use it often:

_____

_____

_____

_____

_____

_____

4.   While in the midst of your next angry mood, and even if you are in the middle of an argument, try to avoid words like "never" or "always". While they may serve to justify your anger, they are inaccurate and exacerbate a situation.

_____

_____

_____

_____

_____

5.   Remember that anger is usually a response to some injustice that you feel you have experienced. While the traumatic event you experienced may have been an extreme injustice, daily slights of life are not necessarily directed at you.

MY LIFE STORY - A NARRATIVE EXERCISE

RECOVERY STORY
FRANK, HEALTH TRAUMA

F RANK, A 32-YEAR-OLD CONSTRUCTION FOREMAN WAS NEVER REALLY SICK A DAY IN HIS LIFE – UNTIL THIS PAST SUMMER. Used to being in the sun, Frank had never really had a problem with exertion or overheating. Extreme tiredness that never seemed to go away and debilitating headaches forced him, though, to consider that maybe he had been working too hard and he visited his doctor for a checkup. The diagnosis of a benign brain tumor came as a complete shock. While his surgery went well and his surgeon assured him he had removed the entire tumor, Frank continued to experience a frightening symptom. He was forgetting the names of the people around him that he had known for years. In fact, he began calling them "Sir" or "Buddy" just to hide his embarrassment at forgetting their names. The stress and anxiety associated with a fear of cancer recurrence, based on this single symptom, began causing Frank sleepless nights. His fears were interfering in his relationship with his wife who tried in vain to reassure him. Exploring what Frank really enjoyed helped bring up a long ago hobby of writing, perfect for this narrative exercise. Reflecting on the steps in the exercise not only served to help him work through the fear at the heart of his diagnosis – that he would not live to see his sons grow up as he faced his mortality – but also put him back in touch with a passion he had long since forgotten.

GOAL

Your goal of the *My Life Story – A Narrative Exercise* is to begin creating emotional distance from your past so that you can become reflective in order to gain perspective on your life as a whole. This is a storytelling outline that helps you organize life events and gain self-compassion, without going too deeply into the memories.

TIME OUT

Always reflect on your inner state and notice if you need a break from the exercise to find your inner calm.

MATERIALS AND LAYOUT

Pen or pencil and the form we have provided on the following pages.

PATH TO COMPLETE

Recounting your story is important for creating coherent episodes from chaotic events. This helps you re-establish a sense of identity as well as gaining some control over feelings of helplessness. We all have complicated lives but few of us take the time to truly know ourselves and so are left with a sense of uncertainty. This exercise opens the door to knowing and appreciating ourselves more deeply. The idea is not to add more than seven to ten words for any title, chapter, or line – or for the section, *Into the Future*. This keeps the exercise more reflective and less emotional, so we can really take over the role of being our own Wise Counsel.

My Life Story

1.   Write your Book Title below:

_____

_____

_____

_____

_____

_____

_____

_____

_____

2.   Write out a minimum of seven Life Chapter Titles below that represent significant life stages and events. For each Chapter, write out one line to describe the Life Chapter (i.e., 1. Life at the Zoo – My family life was always full of excitement when I was growing up as the youngest of six kids):

1. _____

_____

2. _____

_____

3. _____

_____

4. _____

_____

5. _____

_____

6. _____

_____

7. _____

_____

3. Write your final chapter and one line description below for:

Into the Future _____

_____

_____

_____

_____

_____

_____

_____

_____

_____

_____

_____

_____

_____

_____

4.   Add to your chapters as needed:

_____

_____

_____

_____

_____

_____

_____

_____

_____

_____

_____

MOVING ON TO STEP THREE

Moving to the final step in your healing is an exciting and rewarding feeling. You are ready to redefine yourself in your meaningful relationships and in activities you enjoyed previously, or in which you always had an interest. You have determined that, through your hard work and persistence, you are able to care for yourself, to self-soothe and to relax when necessary.

CHAPTER 12 DAILY HABITS FOR STEP 2: REMEMBERING

JUST FOR TODAY

1. Think of one piece of unfinished business that you have as a result of your trauma. Did you put certain plans on hold in your relationships, career, or schooling?

    _____

    _____

    _____

    _____

    _____

    _____

2. Develop a second list of the primary benefits to resolving the unfinished business. What would you gain from returning to school? Taking up the hobby you left behind? Re-igniting your passion for music? We will address this later when we talk about reconnecting as well, but for now, this daily habit serves to help motivate you to remember your trauma, tell your story and realize that reconnecting is your next important step to living again!

    _____

    _____

    _____

    _____

    _____

3.   Make a list of your top three priorities to focus on in regards to your healing. If sitting down to write your story seems overwhelming, a commitment to write a paragraph a day or a two-minute audiotape may be more manageable. Make your steps to healing bite-sized so you can achieve your goals over time.

_____

_____

_____

_____

_____

SECTION 4
STEP 3: BEGINNING TO LIVE AGAIN!

CHAPTER 13 GENTLY MOVING FORWARD WITH LIFE

We need to use our own Wise Counsel to guide us to the best people, places, and vision of our world that is possible. And looking at ourselves in a new light can be a wonderful first step to a new life. This, then, is the purpose of our final section – helping you to use your newfound awareness and insight into how your trauma has affected you and your relationships. We hope you will move toward reconnecting with others and to find your passion for life once again!

GOALS FOR BEGINNING TO LIVE AGAIN!

1.   Redefining yourself within your intimate and social relationships

2.   Addressing the challenges inherent in reconnecting with others

3.   Developing coping skills during your healing process and after

4.   Gaining knowledge into four primary reconnection arenas through physical, intellectual, creative, and personal growth pursuits

5.   Applying your new skills daily

CHAPTER 14 REDEFINING YOURSELF FOLLOWING YOUR TRAUMA

As you address your trauma and begin resolving your emotional symptoms, you may find that you feel freer and lighter - more excited about establishing new relationships and reconnecting with cherished older relationships. In this final phase of recovery, we will focus on establishing or re-establishing meaningful relationships and beginning to live a full life! Gaining closure on your traumatic experience helps you accept that the past events are now part of your history and do not have to define the person you are in the present. You can make decisions today about who you want to be and how you want to live with the resources and opportunities you have right now. This realization alone helps pave the way for building a solid support system through new relationships and enhancing your current ones. In this chapter, we will look at how to redefine yourself within your current intimate relationships and social relationships, as well as redefining yourself as an employee and student following your trauma. We encourage you to enrich your life, taking advantage of new opportunities that await within your widening circle of connections, activities and new interests! First, let us look at the benefits of forgiveness, as this is where the genesis of true healing begins.

THE BENEFITS OF FORGIVENESS

One wise client reminded me recently, that remaining angry is like drinking poison and hoping that it will hurt the person or event that we felt hurt by. Releasing anger is an incredibly freeing experience and one that can improve our feelings of well-being almost immediately. So our focus on forgiveness is more about forgiving ourselves than those we see as harmful toward us. When we reflect on a traumatic event, sometimes we can become highly critical of our actions – blaming ourselves at times for events beyond our control. In many cases, we might recall how an event unfolded and find some small detail that we feel holds the key to the event. We might tell ourselves that either our failure to act or an action we chose to take contributed to a terrible outcome. As an example, one client admitted to blaming herself for leaving her home at 5:00 pm instead of 7:00 pm as an explanation for encountering the dangerous driver. She lost trust in her judgment and concluded that she was not to be trusted or forgiven for some event that was outside of her knowledge or control. In other cases, we may actually have been involved in an activity that was risky and resulted in a trauma. We can use this experience to learn about what drove our behavior and to renew healthier choices in our lives. Without self-forgiveness, this is a difficult task to accomplish. Examining the areas of our lives where we let ourselves down can be extremely fruitful in leading to an entirely different lifestyle, one that is more enriching, safe and satisfying. So what would it take for you to forgive yourself for the times that you feel you have let yourself down? In fact, if you reflect on this deeply you may be surprised at the anger that you carry towards yourself and how this holds you back and limits your life goals.

One client was determined that his employer was responsible for events that led to his job loss. When this individual truly examined the events, he was able to recognize that he tended to become angry with clients over the phone, especially if they seemed to ask a lot of questions about the product he was selling. The employer had noted this behavior on several occasions and suggested that the company would pay for him to attend a customer service course. The individual was annoyed and felt that the manager was targeting him. Eventually, a customer was so insulted that she contacted the company owner resulting in his job loss. When this individual finally reflected on what had occurred, he could see that his anger toward the manager was unreasonable but kept him from focusing on what was generating the angry responses and on the skills development required to do his job well.

He felt so embarrassed that he chose to focus on others rather than to address the source of his anger. The job loss gave him the opportunity to come to terms with his anger and get to the root of it. He learned that he could forgive himself as he realized that his anger toward others came from an upbringing with a parent who would not tolerate any questioning of *authority*. Every time this individual encountered a customer who asked "too many questions," his early childhood encounters with an intolerant parent was ignited. What is the root of your anger towards others and towards yourself? Are you able to find a way to forgive yourself? Remember, we are all imperfect beings and embracing this without anger can actually open the door to learning and self-acceptance – an essential part of our healing. There may indeed be areas where you feel you have let yourself down, put your trust in a person, organization, or system that proved untrustworthy, or simply did not give attention to your actions. If this is the case, it is useful to ask yourself if you have a habit of putting trust in others who are not deserving of this. Do you betray yourself in this way? If you answer yes to this question, it is useful information as it can help you to recognize that there are choices to be made that can only come from awareness of your actions and motivations. It is your right to choose who you trust and to make wise choices for your future, starting today. Finally, carrying anger tends to result in ongoing pain and discomfort. Carrying anger can be an all-consuming experience that steals the energy needed to live. So, if someone injured you or if you blame yourself for something, continuing to hold on to this anger has the unfortunate result of only injuring yourself. Forgiveness means freeing up energy so you can live the best life possible. After all, isn't this the point? It is clear that failing to recover or live well does not improve the situation.

REDEFINING YOUR FAMILY

Family relationships can suffer because of the trauma you have experienced. However, those closest to you can also be the greatest allies in your healing and a tremendous source of strength. We have found that family and friends are an important motivator to *get well* for many of our clients suffering from trauma – they are far more invested in improving the lives of their family and close connections than their own. This is honorable, of course, and speaks to the influence and importance of our closest relationships. First, we will discuss how your family as a whole may be affected by your trauma and then introduce ways in which you can help strengthen your intimate relationship, parenting role, friendship and relations within your family of origin.

HOW YOUR FAMILY MAY BE AFFECTED BY YOUR TRAUMA

Our ability to trust, communicate, and remain intimate with our family can be severely tested following trauma. Man-made traumas, versus natural disasters have been shown to have a longer lasting effect on the ability to enjoy close relationships, due to lingering feelings of betrayal and danger. We feel and behave differently and this has a profound effect on our other family members. Often called into action emotionally and physically to become caregivers following a trauma, many may feel unprepared and incompetent to handle these challenging needs, through no fault of theirs – or yours. Many factors can affect the way in which your family views your trauma, including the severity of your symptoms and the past traumas that each of you experienced in your family of origin. Living with a family member who has PTSD can lead to other members displaying the same symptoms, so we recommend being your own Wise Counsel in determining the effect your trauma has had on your family. Just as in the hard work that you have done thus far, we are here to assure you that you can also enjoy close, loving, intimate relationships again as you gently move forward in your healing. Revisiting the four clusters of symptoms provide clues as to how your family may be affected by your trauma:

- **Re-Experiencing:** The nature of re-experiencing trauma can be disconcerting to you as the trauma survivor, your spouse, and your children. Nightmares or disturbing dreams, intrusive thoughts, images and perceptions of the trauma, dissociative episodes and hallucinations can occur without warning, leaving you feeling upset at their randomness. Witnessing these re-experiencing symptoms can leave your spouse, children, parents, or siblings afraid for your well-being as well as questioning whether you will be able to care for them if needed. The anger that you express towards the trauma itself can be easily misconstrued by your family and cause additional harm.

- **Avoidance and Numbing**: This second cluster of symptoms is among the most common that bring people to family therapy. Avoiding the places, people, or things that remind you of your trauma can serve to cut you off from your family. Withdrawal and an inability to express positive emotions can be perceived by your children and other family members as disinterest or no longer caring about them. The detached numbness of this post-traumatic symptom cluster can lead to withdrawal in social and sexual activities that may be difficult for your family to understand.

- **Negative Cognition and Mood**: A cycle of negative talk results in feelings of self-blame, shame, and self-hatred. Once we are able to break down the negative self-defensive wall we begin making small steps to reconnect with others and feel better our ourselves.

- **Hyperarousal:** Continually being on edge and jumpy can lead to the inability, of course, to relax and enjoy your family and may lead to similar symptoms in them.

HOW TO HELP YOUR FAMILY

Communication and openly sharing your feelings and concerns is critical. Compassion, empathy and respect are the foundation for any family life, and are even more important following a traumatic event. Helping your family through this challenging time is an excellent way to help yourself in the process as well as give meaning to your trauma and the effect it has had on your life. Approach your family with the compassion and empathy that you require in order to heal and the stage will be set for a pattern that is beneficial to you all. Sharing what you have learned in this book such as self-soothing and relaxation techniques can help them now and in the future. As they experience the impact of your trauma, they can also benefit from being a part of your healing. Your family may respond to you in ways that are confusing and difficult for all of you to understand. One such example is sympathy. This is a normal reaction for someone to have towards you as a trauma survivor, however, it may be distressing if you are used to being the caretaker of your family - the *strong* one! The balance between sympathy and empathy must be communicated, as well as awareness of the propensity to rely *too* heavily on your family for your emotional needs so they do not take on the role of therapist. No one likes to see their loved one in pain, however, most of us do not like to be pitied either as this can have a negative effect on our self-esteem. If the people around us do not think we can move past our trauma, we can feel as if we are less competent as well.

REDEFINING YOURSELF AS A PARTNER

Intimacy and sexual problems are two common issues when one partner has PTSD. A shift often takes place following a trauma that will require both of you to make the effort to regain the natural dynamic of your relationship. From the very mundane, such as a redistribution of your daily responsibilities and tasks, to the obligation of being a caregiver, these new ways of relating to one another must be addressed in order to ensure the needs of each of you are met. The commitment to one another may never have been tested quite as strenuously as following a trauma, however, the opportunity for closeness and intimacy, along with a shared sense of having gone through such a tremendous hardship together and having come out stronger is our hope for you.

HOW YOUR PARTNER MAY BE AFFECTED & HOW TO HELP

Depression and a sense of helplessness are a risk to the loved one of a trauma survivor. This is to be expected. Trauma is not planned or anticipated in most cases and each of us processes it differently based on our personality and previous traumas. We may feel a strong desire to be of help but not know the best approach. This may produce a great deal of stress and anxiety for the partner of a trauma survivor. Trauma equals danger, whether or not we experienced it ourselves or secondarily, through a loved one. This loss of feeling safe can lead to depression and anxiety as we sense that we are no longer able to count on the predictability of life. The better you are able to communicate your needs in a compassionate and respectful way, the more able your partner will be to meet those needs. Awareness of your feelings and expressing them in a very honest and open way is the first step towards re-establishing intimacy and closeness. Sharing with your partner the different cluster of symptoms and establishing a type of *shorthand* that the two of you can use exclusively when being triggered or feeling overwhelmed can be a source of comfort for you both – in addition to the sense that you are in this situation together and will get through it together.

REDEFINING YOURSELF AS A PARENT

The same cluster of symptoms that we discussed earlier in the book present challenges for you as a parent with PTSD. One of our goals in helping you redefine yourself as a parent is to keep your trauma from progressing in a generational sense. Recognizing the effects of your trauma on your children and alleviating their stress and anxiety is important in keeping them healthy and moving forward, ensuring that the future generations aren't impacted negatively due to unresolved trauma for any of your family members.

While the risk for secondary traumatization is real, the support and love you provide your children will act as a buffer and reduce the chance of long-term issues. Getting the help you need and managing your symptoms will further enhance your ability to accomplish this. Challenges that children of trauma survivors have shown include emotional responses where they take on the issues of the parent such as nightmares, depression and anxiety. Finally they may suffer from social problems due to an inability to share what is happening within the family and bring home friends, etc.

If you are a parent, it is likely that you have already given thought, or are even anxious about, the effects of your PTSD symptoms on your children. Secondary traumatization *is* seen in children whose parents have suffered trauma, so we will look at how they may be affected and how you can best help them going forward, while also taking gentle care of yourself.

HOW YOUR CHILDREN MAY BE AFFECTED & HOW TO HELP

It is important to explain the reasons behind your feelings and behaviors. Your children are intuitive and sense when you may be in pain, but may not know how, or be able, to ask what is wrong and may even assume they are to blame. The level of detail of your trauma that you share is best assessed by you according to their age and maturity level. In general, while graphic details are not necessary, it is useful to explain that you have not been feeling well due to the event, that it is not their fault or responsibility and that you are working hard to feel better. Children are especially intuitive to the emotions and feelings within the four walls of their home and most often respond in one of three ways:

- **Over-Identifying:** The goal of a child who is over-identifying is to connect with you as a parent. In order to do this, he or she may exhibit the same symptoms that you are exhibiting as the trauma survivor in order to remain close to you.
- **Caretaking:** In an effort to help you through your pain, your child may take on the role of caregiver and try to rescue you. This is taking on the role of the adult and upsetting the natural dynamic of your role as parent.
- **Uninvolved Emotionally:** The sadness and anxiety that may be present in the household is often too much for the child who is uninvolved emotionally, so he or she may disconnect from their feelings and emotions in order to cope.

If your children are having severe emotional or behavioral problems, whether they are caused or exacerbated by, or not even as a result of your trauma, consider therapy with a Family Systems Therapist, specially trained in trauma that can include the entire family. Family therapy can help support you as the trauma survivor while also providing psychoeducation and psychosocial support in helping your family get your needs met. Your own individual trauma therapy at the same time is often a good idea. The best therapeutic approach is determined by the children's age and maturity level: Play therapy is very effective for younger children; talk therapy or expressive therapy for older children and adolescents. Social and behavioral problems and secondary traumatization are a risk for the children in your household. Sharing the reasons behind your feelings and behaviors, without graphic details, and assuring them that they are in no way at fault, can help them integrate the trauma into their history without it becoming intergenerational.

REDEFINING YOURSELF AS A FRIEND

Friends are a tremendous source of support in the face of a traumatic event. The dynamics of a couple or family relationship are not involved in a friendship so we can often lay bare our feelings in a more honest and open way than with a partner. Avoidance and numbing, the second cluster of traumatic symptoms, however, can lead to avoiding social interactions with others, even our closest friends. Following a trauma, the most honest and open thing you can do to reassure your friends is to tell them what you need from them. Educating your close friends on the symptoms of PTSD – and sharing this book with them – can help them understand what you may be going through and your need for safety and social interaction, even when you may be experiencing moodiness or exhibiting quite the opposite. It is important to remain connected to those with whom you have an especially close relationship. Your sense of belonging is a basic human need and isolation can cause further suffering.

REDEFINING YOURSELF AS AN EMPLOYEE/STUDENT

Your employer or teachers may be aware of the traumatic incident if it was a news event, however, sharing a diagnosis of Post-Traumatic Stress Disorder with a boss, or school administrators and teachers can be challenging at best. It may be essential to redefine your role as an employee or a student by notifying Human Resources or your School Administration that your post-trauma symptoms may affect your performance and to reassure them that you have coping strategies in place. Educating those you report to about the symptoms you may be experiencing at a very high level may be helpful in gaining the support that you require. A diagnosis of PTSD is covered under the Americans with Disabilities Act (ADA) and the Family Medical Leave Act (FMLA). Receiving the compassion and empathy you deserve following your trauma promotes your healing.

CHAPTER 15 CHALLENGES IN RECONNECTING WITH OTHERS

As you have seen, our most challenging task in healing is often reconnecting with those people whom we love and care for – our intimate and social relationships. Choosing to rely on others might result in feelings of discomfort. There may be a sense of vulnerability in trusting even the smallest part of ourselves to another. Building trusting relationships with healthy emotional boundaries is a needed element of fully recovering from trauma.

CHOOSING TO RELY ON OTHERS

Choosing to rely on others, particularly after suffering a trauma, is important, and in a way, even enticing. In fact, the idea of someone taking care of us after trauma may feel very appealing. We may feel exhausted and in need of another's care and attention. However, sometimes our connections with others take an odd turn, especially when we experience something as upsetting as a trauma – or even suffer the effects of it years later (often because of an unrelated event). There are questions that we can ask ourselves about what is happening in our relationships and whether there are problems or we are receiving the support we need. Consider the following:

- What is your social support?
- Whom do you feel closest to and feel you can count on?
- How often do you see them?
- Do you feel as if there is a pattern of relationship problems amongst your friends or family that you'd like to resolve?
- Has this been going on for some time?
- If there are issues, could they be related to some behavior that comes up when you are together? Have you been quicker to anger and feel as if you have a short temper since the trauma or retriggering of an old trauma?

- Are you a member of any organization, group, or affiliated with any religious or spiritual groups?
- Have you kept up this affiliation or let it lapse?
- Would you like to form a reconnection now?
- Are you close with children no longer living in your home?
- Do you have hobbies or interests that have fallen by the wayside?
- Would you like to re-ignite this passion?
- Have you changed your social needs and obligations since your trauma?
- How has this made you feel?

We need a social support system, but the quality of these relationships is of utmost importance, not simply the quantity. The possibility of attaching ourselves in an unhealthy manner is inherent in trauma which we will discuss in a moment.

ATTACHMENT DISORDER

Attachment theory describes the dynamics of our long-term, intimate relationships, and while our attachment styles form in early infancy, they extend into adulthood and our intimate relationships in the display of four styles of attachment to one another:

- Secure
- Anxious-Preoccupied
- Dismissive-Avoidant and
- Fearful-Avoidant

Our attachment to others begins early in life. Our social interactions are integrated and coordinated with each other and when this falls short or this normal, secure attachment is disturbed, the outcome is truly heart-rending and chilling.

There is a famous experiment conducted by Dr. Edward Tronick of the University of Massachusetts, Boston known as the Still Face Baby Experiment that perfectly illustrates the raw, primal effects of our attachment to others – or rather our distress and terror when that attachment is disturbed. In his experiment, Dr. Tronick instructs the mother of a year-old baby girl to play and engage with her. The mother is then instructed to completely disconnect and become completely still-faced, showing no emotion. The baby tries desperately to engage her mother, becoming confused and extremely distressed at her lack of attention and positive feedback. When the experiment ends after just a minute or two and the mother begins again to reconnect with her daughter, the baby is able to return quite quickly to her previous state. For many children, however, significant people in their lives, their primary caregivers, create a stressful environment where the opportunity for healthy attachment does not even exist. This disconnection often extends into adult relationships becoming a way of life and a method of relating, causing enduring stress.

ATTACHMENT TO YOUR THERAPIST

Attachments often form with the one significant person who initially accepts the trauma survivor, without judgment and with a whole and open connection. In some cases this can be with a skilled trauma therapist. The therapeutic bond is a unique one not found in any other relationship with another person. A connection with the therapist is the first step in forming the bond. Compassion is a requirement of the relationship, as is empathy and understanding. However, growth is also a goal of therapy, and for this to happen, an authentic, true bond must exist. The therapist must truly care about her client in order to model a healthy relationship where her client can gain insight and flourish into the person he or she was meant to be. Every client has the option of simply not coming back, week after week, but establishing a connection is the important first step to making sure therapy is a success. With a bond this significant, the risk of attachment also exists. Who among us wants to leave someone who so completely accepts us? Trauma survivors who have experienced abuse in their childhood may be particularly susceptible and if this is an issue, please feel comfortable in bringing this concern to your therapist's attention so he or she may help you through the process of forming a healthy connection with others by modeling a productive relationship with you. The ultimate goal is to help you realize that there are others who are ready and willing to accept you without judgment and with a whole and open connection.

TRUSTING YOUR CHOICES

Forming healthy attachments is the ultimate test in trusting your choices, but none of us has a crystal ball. We cannot foretell what another person will, or will not do, in the course of a relationship. We can only do our best to establish our boundaries, state them clearly, and remain aware of when they are being disrespected. For those with difficulty establishing and maintaining boundaries, the protective factor of a healthy relationship is missing. Boundary setting is important in life, and in our relationships. It is critical that we determine what hurts us, what heals us, what empowers us, what makes us feel good – what we deserve from others, and what we do not. The second important part of this, of course, is communicating that to those who overstep our boundaries. Challenges continue during our healing and beyond.

In the next chapter, we discuss coping skills that you can master in handling stress and loneliness and look at the hurtful habits that we sometimes employ.

CHAPTER 16 COPING DURING HEALING & BEYOND

Even after healing, stressors still exist in life. In fact, as you have learned, pain is a part of life. However, there are strategies you can employ to make stressors, including feelings of loneliness just a bit easier to bear. Also, we will introduce the concept of the use of life strategies (or Hurtful Habits) that tend to work against our best interests. Since you are working toward getting stronger and resolving your trauma history, it is important to challenge habits that might be hindering your progress. This, then, is a part of your gentle journey and of calling on your ability to find comfort, no matter what stage of your healing.

COPING WITH STRESS

Stressors exist in life – there is no escape and, as a trauma survivor, you may feel especially vulnerable when faced with additional demands. However, with the self-soothing and relaxation skills that you have learned in healing from your trauma, you're well ahead of others in being able to confidently handle any stress that does come your way. As you become stronger and more self-confident both during and following your healing, you will be able to call on the skills that you have learned to accept and cope with the psychosocial and environmental stressors that we experience at one point or another, including:

- Grief:
  Grief and loss are the most severe of stressors that include the death of a spouse or loved one, family member or close friend.
- Family:
  Family issues include behavioral and educational difficulties with children, separation, divorce, remarriage, a change in living conditions such as becoming a caregiver for an elderly parent that places additional stress on the family.

- Financial:

  From severe such as abject poverty to temporary such as the loss of a job, and thus a dependable source of income, financial stress is one of the most insidious and disconcerting stressors for families.

- Occupational:

  Aside from job loss, addressed above, which relates to financial stress, occupational challenges include personality differences with your supervisor or co-workers, job dissatisfaction, stressful schedules or conditions, the threat of an impending layoff or planned retirement.

This is but a short list of stressors, but when any of these do occur (not *if*, because they happen to us all at one time or another!) you will be able to revisit your self-soothing and relaxation exercises to ward off the physiological and emotional symptoms, or even triggers, before they happen.

Gaining awareness of your feelings, particularly during times of stress, is helpful so that you can determine how to best proceed. Putting a name to your feelings is an excellent first step.

PTSD is an anxiety disorder. To determine if your feelings (anger, for example) are related to your PTSD or are simply a reaction that anyone might experience, ask yourself the following to gain a sense of whether your feelings are anxiety-related:

- *Am I in danger right now?*
- *If not, is my worrying out of proportion to what I'm experiencing?*
- *Am I worrying about things excessively?*
- *Are others telling me I'm worrying excessively?*

COPING WITH LONELINESS

Traumatic Loneliness is a special kind of loneliness that develops among trauma survivors. Aside from the loneliness that is part of the human condition, as a trauma survivor, you may feel that your experience with trauma has isolated you from others adding to your burden. The effect of loneliness itself can result in the feeling of being re-traumatized because the effect of social isolation can include increased feelings of depression and anxiety. If we have begun to withdraw socially because we do not feel safe among others, then this will further impair our ability to connect and get our much needed support.

There are a number of features to this concept of Traumatic Loneliness that we will review in a moment. There is a propensity on the part of trauma survivors to protect those whom they love from the horrors that they endured or the pain they continue to feel. As you can imagine, this only serves to deepen the feelings of loneliness and isolation. Most loved ones, however, would welcome the opportunity to help and are much stronger than imagined. This is the time to draw upon their strength and to share with those whom you feel safe. Picture, if you will, someone whom you love coming to you asking if he or she could talk. In the best case, you would try to welcome them into your heart and encourage them to talk and even allow them to cry. You deserve no less. Although you have already taken a long journey in your road to recovery and have begun reconnecting with those who are special to you and with whom you want to have a significant relationship, there are times in all our lives when we suffer from loneliness.

Loneliness from social isolation – even self-imposed - leads to a higher propensity for depression, a feeling that we are unworthy of the relationships that we *do* have, and feelings of emptiness and despair. A serious loss of self-esteem can result.

Loneliness can also occur due to a lack of intimate relationships, because, again it's the quality and intimacy in a relationship that gives it its depth and meaning. Simply having many friends isn't the key to alleviating feelings of loneliness. Your self-soothing skills are especially helpful if you feel the pain of loneliness approaching.   Pay particular attention to those that resonate with you. Acknowledge the loneliness you feel when it arises as this is an important first step in gaining awareness and insight into your healthy and reasonable need for connection.

If you are continuing to have difficulties connecting with others, the possibility exists that you may be thinking in ways that may no longer be in your best interest, leading to greater feelings of loneliness, such as:

- *I learned that life and people are dangerous*
- *I do not trust my choices*
- *I may relate to others but I have no one who is close to me*
- *Attachments are unhealthy*
- *My thinking about my relationships is disorganized; I'm not sure where I stand with people important to me*
- *When people aren't close to me, it makes me feel sad*
- *I have a sense of being distanced from myself internally which makes it hard for me to relate to others*
- *Life is chaotic; I can't trust that things will change or ever be "better"*
- *I was traumatized when I was young, so it's hard to connect and fully trust another person*
- *My destiny is to remain lonely*
- *I'm independent – I can depend on myself for this, but not others*
- *I choose not to rely on others*
- *There is a huge risk of betrayal in making connections with others*
- *It's safer to be alone than to risk the unknown or betrayal, hurt, or rejection*
- *No one understands me or my need to be alone*
- *Human beings are lonely*
- *I'm not willing to make the effort, and then still be lonely*
- *Social media more than meets my needs! (Hint: Facebook relationships don't count as connections!)*
- *I'm like Clint Eastwood, the strong, silent, independent type – I don't need people*
- *I've never connected with people. How would I even begin when I don't know how?*

- *I've learned to be alone*

HURTFUL HABITS

Once we have worked hard to stabilize and work through the impact of trauma, we may notice that we are still not doing as well as we had hoped. This may not have to do with the trauma you experienced but rather with habits that continue to hinder your ability to live the best life that you can.

The list below is useful in keeping you on track in your goal to a full recovery and a rich and engaging life. Everyone struggles with hurtful habits from time to time – friends, family, and even the both of us struggle with these habits. So the following is a reminder to keep us from getting stuck in a thinking loop that we cannot disengage from no matter what we try. Whenever you notice that you are not moving forward in your life or that you continue to struggle even though the trauma no longer feels as intense, read through this list and notice where your stumbling blocks lie.   Are you inclined to one of the habits below – or a number of them? What would you like to do to challenge this? And is it a compulsion to help avoid anxiety, or an impulse, more out of habit?

- Complaining: About our work, families, spouses, and friendships
- Wasting Time: Worrying about wasting time
- Self-Deception: Not being honest with yourself; not facing your own faults
- Knowing what is good for you, then NOT doing it
- Worrying about things that will not happen
- Not preparing for things that will happen
- Resistance to change
- Addiction to substances
- Addiction to negative people
- Addiction to bad attitudes
- Tendency to engage in harmful activities

- Being nice to everyone but yourself
- Minimizing your achievements
- Wanting other's approval more than your own
- Not following your dreams
- Insufficient nourishment for your body; i.e., exercise, diet, water
- Losing energy through hate and anger
- Inaccurate self-perceptions that you refuse to release
- Presuming that others see you as negatively as you see yourself
- Defending an irrational position
- Wondering when to begin instead of just doing it; assuming that you have begun
- Not living the moment
- Pretending: No one fakes well in front of animals!

CHAPTER 17 EXERCISES FOR STEP 3: BEGINNING TO LIVE AGAIN!

FOUR KEYS TO RECONNECTING WITH LIFE

The exercises we will introduce in this third and final phase of recovery help you redefine yourself in terms of your meaningful relationships and engage in social activities that you either once enjoyed, or that you would like to try! One of the most empowering aspects of healing from trauma is the realization that your trauma does not need to define you as a person. Through these exercises, we hope that you experience a widening circle of connections and that you will have the opportunity to explore a depth of interests that enrich your life. Along with redefining yourself following your trauma, both personally and within your significant relationships, the opportunity to pursue pleasure again may be just what you need. As you begin to experience real progress in your healing, you may find that the patterns you have developed to cope with your symptoms are no longer necessary and that you would like to begin socializing and connecting with others – to begin living again! As in the exercises found in *Step One: Finding Comfort* and *Step Two: Remembering Your Trauma*, we introduce you to a client who has benefitted from the exercise, as well as the goals, time out, the materials and layout, and the instructions to complete the exercise. The following is a list of exercises developed for *Section 3: Beginning to Live Again!*

- Physical Connections
- Intellectual Connections
- Creative and Artistic Pursuits
- Spiritual and Personal Growth

PHYSICAL CONNECTIONS EXERCISE

RECOVERY STORY
JOANNA, VIOLENCE IN HER MARRIAGE

JOANNA COPED WITH THE END OF HER MARRIAGE BY TURNING TO FOOD FOR COMFORT. The constant verbal attacks that she suffered left her with little self-esteem and no real way to reclaim the person she once was. She turned to food as a means of stuffing down her retorts to her husband, knowing that failing to do this would mean his attacks would become more vicious. During therapy, she discussed, what she called, her "before" life. She had been a physical person as a teen, competing in and winning a number of track and field meets while in high school. While she felt totally out of shape physically, she was also able to identify her previous accomplishments as a source of pride and self-esteem that she had not felt since being married. The urge to reclaim that feeling was one that drove her to examine different physical pursuits, more in keeping with where she was in her life after her divorce. As a parent to two teens, she was not ready to commit to a training regimen of running, but she had always been interested in yoga and was curious about what it entailed. Joanna signed up and paid for three classes. In her mind, she felt that, since she had paid for them, she had provided herself with a level of commitment to give them a go, as she would be embarrassed to ask for her money back. Incredibly sore and tired after the first class, she admitted that although it was hard, she felt a sense of accomplishment in just getting through it – it was much more difficult than she had imagined.

After relaxing during the week, Joanna found herself looking forward to the next class and meeting up with another woman she spoke with at the first class. Joanna found that opening her mind to a new experience gave her the courage and commitment (after all, it was only three classes – she could do it!) to try something that she previously would not have even considered – and ended up truly enjoying.

GOAL

The goal of the *Physical Connections Exercise* is to explore physical ways in which you can connect with others on a more personal and enjoyable level such as joining a walking club, taking up yoga, or signing up for a bowling league. Tai Chi and Qi-gong are also useful and gentle ways to increase our activity levels slowly. As with the three other *connecting* exercises we will address (Intellectual, Creative & Artistic and Spiritual & Personal Growth), our goal through this exercise is to help you settle into your skin and to begin the process of becoming fully and genuinely who you wish to be.

TIME OUT

Always reflect on your inner state and notice if you need a break from the exercise to find your inner calm.

MATERIALS AND LAYOUT

Pen or pencil and the form we have provided on the following pages.

PATH TO COMPLETE

1.   Identify below several physical activities that interest you or that you always wanted to try, such as joining a walking club, taking a yoga class, or joining a bowling league. The activity must include some level of social interaction or element.

_____

_____

_____

_____

_____

_____

2.   Investigate physical activity pursuits that are available in your vicinity, or create your own group!

_____

_____

_____

_____

_____

3.   Based on your investigation, select two to three ways to become involved socially, at least once each month.

_____

_____

_____

_____

_____

_____

_____

4.   Decide if any one of these activities is a good fit for you after attending at least three to four times. If this particular activity is not a good fit, move on to the next!

_____

_____

_____

_____

_____

INTELLECTUAL CONNECTIONS EXERCISE

D ANIEL WAS A 62-YEAR-OLD SECURITY CHIEF AT A REGIONAL MALL WHO WITNESSED ONE OF HIS TOWN'S WORST MASS SHOOTINGS. The trauma he suffered was extremely complex in that he not only lost friends and colleagues in the incident, but he felt a heightened sense of responsibility for the safety of his staff and the mall patrons. As a Vietnam Vet who had served in the Special Forces and law enforcement after coming home, he had seen his share of tragedies, however, this incident left him drained, depressed and continually questioning why he was spared his life. Prior to the incident, and as retirement became imminent, Daniel began experiencing a sense of approaching change. He knew that physically he was unable to respond to the needs of the job as he had previously and was looking forward to pursuits that were more intellectual. The continual physical training through his career required him to be in great shape, but still, he looked forward to not being pushed to his physical limits. In completing this exercise, he was able to explore his interests, both in terms of integrating the trauma into his history and moving his life in a new direction.

Daniel was thrilled to learn that a university in his town offered free courses to residents over 60. While his initial instinct was to take courses in law enforcement, he stayed on task with the exercise and selected courses that he simply had interest in, with no particular goal, like career development, in mind. Archeology held particular interest for him and he decided to attend a number of classes, eventually becoming a volunteer docent at the Natural History Museum. While the trauma remained a source of pain for him, its intensity slowly dissipated as he widened his social circle and expanded his interests, eventually becoming a paid employee of the Museum – and for the first time, not in security.

GOAL

The goal of the *Intellectual Connections Exercise* is to help you expand your interests, and perhaps, explore entirely new areas of intellectual pursuits. Opportunities are abound in life and it is never too late to nurture your growth and to accomplish a higher level of thinking – and being.

TIME OUT

Always reflect on your inner state and notice if you need a break from the exercise to find your inner calm.

MATERIALS AND LAYOUT

Pen or pencil and the form we have provided on the following pages.

PATH TO COMPLETE

1.   Investigate the sources of intellectual pursuits in your area. Some places you may want to look include universities and libraries. Join intellectual groups such as chess club or book clubs, or create your own! List some ideas below:

_____

_____

_____

_____

2.   Select two to three ways to become socially involved with others, at least once each month:

_____

_____

_____

_____

3.   Decide if any one of these activities is a good fit for you only after attending at least three to four times. If it is not a good fit, move on to the next!

_____

_____

_____

_____

_____

CREATIVE & ARTISTIC PURSUITS EXERCISE

RECOVERY STORY
MAY, GENERATIONAL TRAUMA

MAY, A 47-YEAR-OLD CORPORATE RECRUITER AND MOTHER OF TWO, WATCHED THE NEWS IN HORROR OF A FIRE THAT CLAIMED THE LIFE OF TWO YOUNG CHILDREN. Transported to the moment she heard the news that her twin sister was in a coma and her two young nieces had perished in a fire, she became dizzy, lightheaded and nauseous. It had been 20 years since she attended her nieces' funeral and visited her sister in the hospital – and 17 since they finally removed her from life support. Yet, it seemed like yesterday. Her father had never fully recovered from his favorite granddaughter's death, becoming a shell of his previous self. Indeed, every family gathering, every birthday, every graduation of the other grandchildren felt like a reminder of their loss. Certainly, she reasoned, she had *"gotten over it"* by now.

While she had heard of other deaths since then, of course, these two triggered a sense of loss and depression that she could not shake. During therapy, she uncovered the fact that, though her family had never talked about this trauma that they shared – classic avoidance – none had ever fully recovered. Integrating this trauma into her life, instead of continuing to avoid even thinking about it, became May's mission as she realized that not only had she changed her own behavior, but had passed along the anxiety to her own daughters as well. Words did not come easily to May. She came from a family that was distant at best, in fact, she reflected on the fact that the only person her father had shown affection to was his granddaughter who had passed away. Neither she nor her other siblings received any affection at all.

She realized that what she needed to express was beyond words and she began to explore creative outlets. She found that writing did not help her express her thoughts any more effectively than talk therapy; a mild case of Adult Attention Deficit Disorder (ADD) coupled with the anxiety that she was experiencing only heightened her inability to focus. So, she explored a number of other creative pursuits, including joining a pottery class and taking an art class. She began getting rather frustrated when none of these worked out initially for her – she was too invested in the outcome of the art itself, instead of simply enjoying it for what it was, a search for a creative activity that would help calm her and allow her to express her feelings in a new way. Stumbling upon a jewelry-making class at a craft store one day and having faithfully stayed with the exercise, she promised to give it a chance. She loved it! Not only did she enjoy the fact that the activity itself simply seemed to remove her stress but she enjoyed the social aspect of seeing the other students in the class each week. She was able to find beauty in the pieces that she designed. Something she realized she had not experienced in quite some time and silently dedicated the first three to her sister and her nieces.

GOAL

The goal of the *Creative Pursuits Exercise* is to explore creative outlets for your self-expression and to find activities that truly make you happy and perhaps even help you find your passion!

TIME OUT

Always reflect on your inner state and notice if you need a break from the exercise to find your inner calm.

MATERIALS AND LAYOUT

Pen or pencil and the form we have provided on the following pages.

PATH TO COMPLETE

1.   Search for creative outlets available in your community. There are lots of classes that are free or offered for a nominal fee that may be just what you are seeking. Join a pottery or painting class, a scrapbooking club, or a jewelry class as May did. Resolve to attend at least three to four of these classes to see if it resonates with you. List some ideas below:

_____

_____

_____

_____

2.   Select two to three ways to become socially involved with others, at least once each month. If your original choices are not to your liking, try another and another until you find a creative outlet that speaks to you. Perhaps it is gardening or music – something that allows you to gain a state of relaxation and calm while expressing yourself creatively.

_____

_____

_____

_____

_____

3.   Decide if any one of these activities is a good fit for you only after attending at least three to four times. If it's not a good fit, move on to the next! Explore how you can creatively honor the traumatic event such as May did in creating and dedicating her first three pieces to her sister and nieces. Provide your art with the meaning of what the experience meant to you and allow it to be an integral part of your healing.

SPIRITUAL & PERSONAL GROWTH EXERCISE

RECOVERY STORY
SIOBHAN, SURVIVED HEART ATTACK

IOBHAN, A 58-YEAR-OLD SCHOOL ADMINISTRATOR, EXPERIENCED A HEART ATTACK, ONE IN WHICH SHE NEARLY DID NOT SURVIVE. She was aware that her health had been suffering during a long, stressful divorce process. Sleep was restless when she was even able to fall asleep and coffee was pretty much all that got her through the day. She had felt her heart racing on more than one occasion but felt it was probably due to anxiety – and was too busy, in any case, to take time to figure it all out. Completely overwhelmed and running on empty, she suffered the classic signs of a heart attack one day while at work and was transported to the hospital after quick thinking by her colleagues.

Her recovery was somewhat difficult, but not overly so. It was not until she was released from the hospital and recovering at home, that Siobhan began to realize that she needed real change in her life. She realized she had been in panic mode prior to her heart attack at the demands of her impending divorce. Financially, she had real concerns. With two children in college and the burden of their education falling directly on her, she had to face the reality of delaying her retirement plans and face at least another ten years of work. Emotionally, she was in grief from the loss of her marriage and, along with the aging issues that she faced, realized this was not what she had imagined for her life. Now, in facing her recovery, she added to her already stressful life, another source of anxiety surrounding her physical and emotional health. Very practical matters hounded her: Would she be *able* to work longer? Would she be lonely from here on and be single for the rest of her life? And very practical matters also plagued her: What if she had been alone when she had her heart attack? And could she have another? Siobhan began this exercise in earnest, feeling she had no other choice but to take the reins of her life once more. She had come to the realization that she was in living life in a reactive, passive mode rather than as an active participant, almost as if she were letting life run her and this *wasn't* the way she intended to go forward. With new resolve, she took several weeks to give serious thought to all the questions and to reflect on the answers that led her to a new career direction. As a teacher starting out, she quickly moved up the management ladder, but with each move further away from the children she loved, found that she enjoyed her job less and less. This exercise helped her find her passion once again and take the control of her career choices and, with this, her anxiety began to slowly fade.

GOAL

Our goal with the *Spiritual & Personal Growth Exercise* is to help you identify new ways to help feed your soul, beginning with defining who you are and the *script* you may be following. It is important to identify the repetitive patterns of thoughts and behaviors that keep you doing things in the same way and that keep you back from stepping outside the box to discover what your passions are and to expand your thinking into new areas

TIME OUT

Always reflect on your inner state and notice if you need a break from the exercise to find your inner calm.

MATERIALS AND LAYOUT

Pen or pencil and the form we have provided on the following pages.

PATH TO COMPLETE

1.   It is often difficult to see our own value, our own impact on the world at large, so begin this exercise by trying to see yourself through the eyes of someone whom you love and admire. What do they think of you? What are the gifts that they feel you have given to them?   How would they remember you if you were no longer here?

_____

_____

_____

_____

_____

_____

2.   What are five ways in which their lives are different because you were in it?

_____

_____

_____

_____

_____

_____

3.   Try to imagine yourself at a younger age (five to 20 years ago). What fed your soul before you had responsibilities like a career and a family? What could you do for hours without even giving it a second thought and without regard to income for your activity?

_____

_____

_____

_____

_____

_____

_____

4. What is your true purpose for being here? What would feed your soul now? Exploring your spirituality by joining a religious order, church or temple? Learning to meditate or to getting in touch with nature? Performing community service by volunteering at a homeless shelter? Take time to reflect on the gifts you feel you have to offer the world and how to best provide them. Decide if any one of these activities is a good fit for you only after attending at least three to four times. If it's not a good fit, move on to the next! List at least five activities of a spiritual or personal growth nature that you would like to explore:

_____

_____

_____

_____

_____

_____

MOVING ON FROM STEP THREE

Pain is a necessary part of life but we can also gain insight into our strengths as we integrate this pain into the perspective of our lives as a whole. When this pain is visited through a trauma, it is often helpful to find meaning in our experience. As you move forward in your healing, you may find periods of loneliness and doubt but this is a time for your growth and development as a person. Use it to stretch yourself beyond your expectations, harnessing your efforts to create more meaning, depth, passion, and self-compassion.

CHAPTER 18 DAILY HABITS FOR STEP 3: BEGINNING TO LIVE AGAIN!

JUST FOR TODAY

1.   Ask yourself, *"What can I do today, tomorrow and the next day and the next, to realize happiness in my life?"*

2.   Do you have dreams you have put on hold since your trauma? Remind yourself of these dreams daily and reinforce their importance by answering the following: What are the details of these dreams? Do they relate to the way in which you express yourself, such as writing or creating art? If you took action right now to make these dreams part of your daily life, how would your life change?

3.   You have the freedom of choice. You can choose to do whatever you like, whenever you like. You can choose how to spend the rest of today and tomorrow and the next day after that for the rest of your life. You may not have had control during your traumatic event but you are in control now. What are you going to do with this precious gift of time and freedom?

SECTION 5
WRAPPING UP & MOVING FORWARD

CHAPTER 19 CONCLUSION

What does it really mean to heal from trauma? What can you expect at this stage? Are you really finished with this work? These are all good questions at this time and certainly one that we hear from our clients after working through their trauma history.

Knowing ourselves deeply, gaining personal insight, becoming our own wise counsel are gifts along the road of our personal journey. These are all life enhancing but if we are suffering and struggling with PTSD, we want to and need to get to a place where our traumatic experiences are not the main guiding force in our decisions and our goals.

One of the strongest indicators of trauma recovery is noticing that we are embracing new life experiencing and relationships (both new and old). Making new plans, finding joy in simple things, releasing into this moment and feeling calm all demonstrate fruitful signs of recovery.

We believe that we are wired for recovery and always moving in this direction – sometimes we just need to get out of our own way and take courageous steps toward new and fulfilling life adventures.

Right now my garden is filled with flowers. It is pretty lush but quite messy with splashes of color everywhere. I notice the fragility of the flower petals and recognize that they only come out when they are ready and cannot be forced to fully emerge one moment quicker then when the time is right. Then I think of trauma again and how we are all so fragile but also fully potent with life and light as well. We cannot be rushed either, but with the right ingredients – we fully flower within our own time.

We believe in your right to move in your own time toward healing. Pay attention to what you need right now and add whatever ingredients are essential to your own recovery. You are unique and as you learn to pay attention, you can become very skilled at recognizing what you need right now to take your next step.

Since we see story as a crucial component of healing from trauma, we invite you to share your Trauma Recovery Story with us at www.whatisptsd.com. You can submit your Recovery Story (video or written) for review and posting to our website. We feel that each Recovery Story has the potential to offer the hope of healing for another.

Contact Us form to submit your video or written Recovery Story.

And remember, there is help if you need it. You are not alone. Best wishes on your healing journey!

Anna & Teresa

Visit www.whatisptsd.com for:

- Resources

- Exercise Templates

- Forms

- Information about help in your area

- New products

- Services

- More Recovery Stories

INDEX

Printed in Great Britain
by Amazon

36135169R00129